101 Things You Didn't Know about CASINO GAMBLING

101 Things You Didn't Know about CASINO GAMBLING

Cover Your Ass, Befriend Lady Luck,
and Beat the House
... Every Time

Justin Cord Hayes

Adams Media
Avon, Massachusetts

To my wife, Nicole, for being my lady luck for 10 wonderful years.

Published by Adams Media, an F+W Publications Company
57 Littlefield Street
Avon, MA 02322
www.adamsmedia.com

1-59337-367-8

Printed in Canada.
J I H G F E D C B A

Contains portions of material adapted and abridged from *The Everything® Casino Gambling Book, 1st Edition* by George Mandos, ©1998, Adams Media and *The Everything® Casino Gambling Book, 2nd Edition* by Meg Elaine Schneider, ©2004, F+W Publications, Inc.

Library of Congress Cataloging-in-Publication Data
Hayes, Justin Cord.
101 things you didn't know about casino gambling : cover your ass, befriend lady luck, and beat the house every time / by Justin Cord Hayes.
p.   cm.
ISBN 1-59337-367-8
1. Gambling. 2. Casinos. I. Title.

GV1301.H39 2005
795--dc22
2005026436

This publication is designed to provide accurate and authoritative information with regard to the subject matter covered. It is sold with the understanding that the publisher is not engaged in rendering legal, accounting, or other professional advice. If legal advice or other expert assistance is required, the services of a competent professional person should be sought.
—From a *Declaration of Principles* jointly adopted by a Committee of the American Bar Association and a Committee of Publishers and Associations

This book is available at quantity discounts for bulk purchases.
For information, please call 1-800-872-5627.

I want to take an opportunity to thank Paula Munier, editor extraordinaire, for believing in me from the very beginning. Thanks also to Andrea Mattei for helping me shape this book. Thank you to my family for encouragement and to my colleagues for suggestions.

ACKNOWLEDGMENTS

Contents

Introduction:
The most fun you'll ever have losing money **xiv**

PART 1:
YOU BET YOUR LIFE: BASIC GAMBLING, BASIC STRATEGIES, AND MONEY MANAGEMENT 1

PART 2:
TURNS OF FRIENDLY CARDS: CARD GAMES 27

LOUNGE ACT:
VIVA LAS VEGAS . . . WHAT YOU DIDN'T KNOW ABOUT THE HISTORY OF SIN CITY 80

PART 3:
ROLLING BONES AND BETTING ON BLACK: CRAPS AND ROULETTE 95

LOUNGE ACT:
WHAT ARE THE ODDS? . . . WHAT YOU DIDN'T KNOW ABOUT VEGAS SHOWS 120

PART 4:
BANDITS AND ONSCREEN JOKERS: SLOTS AND VIDEO POKER 135

LOUNGE ACT:
DON'T BET ON IT . . . WHAT YOU DIDN'T KNOW ABOUT LAS VEGAS LANDMARKS AND EVENTS 156

PART 5:
Sucker Bets and Games with Balls: Bingo, Keno, Wheel of Fortune and Others 171

LOUNGE ACT:
Gambling Is Everywhere . . . What You Didn't Know about the Spread of Gambling 204

PART 6:
BE A SPORT: SPORTSBOOK AND HORSERACING 221

LOUNGE ACT:
THE BIG CASINO . . . WHAT YOU DIDN'T KNOW ABOUT DEATH IN VEGAS AND VEGAS-RELATED DEATH 241

"You can-
not beat a roulette
table unless you steal
money from it."
-Albert Einstein

"A dollar picked
up in the road is more
satisfaction to us than the
ninety-nine we had to work for,
and the money won at Faro or in
the stock market snuggles into
our hearts in the same way."
—Mark Twain

"Even as I
approach the gambling
hall, as soon as I hear, two
rooms away, the jingle of the
money poured out on the table, I
almost go into convulsions."
—Fyodor Dostoevsky

INTRODUCTION

The most fun you'll ever have losing money

Little old ladies do it. Virile young men do it. Heck, even birds and bees probably do it. Gambling is a multibillion-dollar industry, and it's available in various forms across forty-eight of the fifty states. And even though it's usually associated with at least a few of the seven deadlies, many a new church wing has been paid for with proceeds from bingo night. Gambling has built great cities as well. Let's face it—Las Vegas would not even exist if the state of Nevada hadn't legalized gambling in 1931, but it remains the nation's fastest-growing metropolis. It's one of the few multinamed cities known to all by just one word: Vegas! (Although that's usually followed by the word "baby.") You don't hear folks saying Francisco!, Antonio!, or Angeles!, now do you?

In *101 Things You Didn't Know about Casino Gambling*, you'll learn a lot about Vegas, baby, and plenty more. Within these pages, you'll also find information on the history of favorite games of chance, tips on how to succeed at them, and sucker bets to avoid in the casino. Sure, some folks make a living from the tables, but most—including you, probably—are casual, novice gamblers looking to get lucky. Well then, you're already in luck, because this book is for you. You'll pick up some strategies that will increase your chances of being a winner. Nevertheless, if you already are a card shark, this book still has plenty to tickle your fancy. You might not know that the King of Rock 'n' Roll was a total flop during his first engagement in Sin City. Or, if all you know about Las Vegas is castles, volcanoes, and dancing fountains, then you'll be surprised to learn how America's adult playground grew from a train stop at an oasis into a city of nearly 2,000,000 people.

This book is divided into six sections: gambling basics and money management, card games, table games, slots and video poker, sucker bets, and sportsbook and horseracing. But in between you'll find several mini-chapters called "lounge acts" because no gambling experience is complete—especially if you're gambling in Las Vegas—unless you take in a lounge act or two. These entertaining inter-chapters focus on the history of Las Vegas, interesting tidbits about Vegas acts, unusual events in Las Vegas history, the rise of gambling outside of Sin City, and even death in Vegas.

So, shake up a martini. Put on some Sinatra. And get ready to roll them bones, turn friendly cards, and learn *101 Things You Didn't Know about Casino Gambling.*

PART 1:

You Bet Your Life:
Basic Gambling, Basic Strategies,
and Money Management

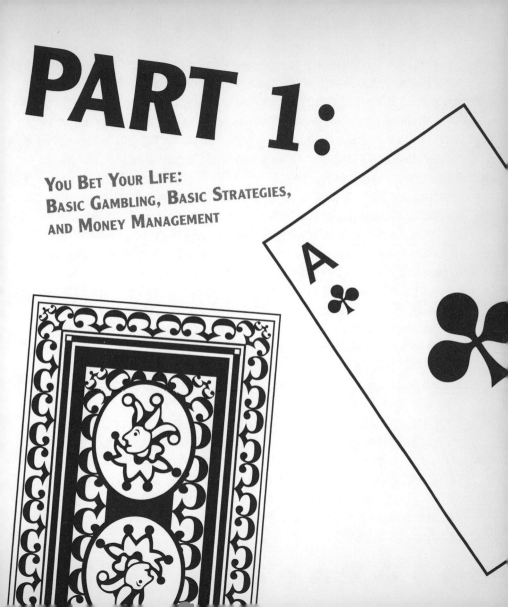

MOST LIKELY, the earliest cave dwellers enjoyed rudimentary forms of gambling. Maybe they took bets on which saber-tooth tiger would be the first to finish devouring a three-toed sloth. Whatever the case may be, wagering on anything and everything just seems to be human nature. If it's true today, then it's probably been true as long as humans have walked erect. So, first you need to get a taste of gambling's long, sometimes sordid past—a past filled with everything from pharaohs to human sacrifices.

Then you'll learn a little bit about odds, the cornerstone of gambling, before turning to the psychological pitfalls strewn within casinos like quagmires of quicksand. From the moment you walk into a casino, you're played like a fiddle. If you know that, then you'll be more likely to avoid subtle tricks that casinos use to get a grip on your wallet or purse.

After a warning about so-called sure-fire gambling strategies, you'll take a ride on the gambling superhighway. Online gambling is a popular way to gamble without leaving your favorite easy chair and without having to interact with other human beings. You won't get comps or free drinks at home, but you can learn how to play your choice games of chance before heading into bricks-and-mortar casinos and throwing down chunks of your life savings. But you've got to be careful as you travel down the online highway, because it too can be a mess of potholes.

Finally, you'll get a feel for some strategies that can help you lose less money. That you'll lose money is pretty much a given when it comes to gambling, because the odds on every single table game and slot machine favor the house. And thanks to some of that psychological mumbo-jumbo casinos employ, you're likely to give all your money back to the house even if you win big. If you go into a gambling palace armed with some foreknowledge, then you'll have a good time gambling, win or lose.

1:
Tumbling dice in Ur:
A very short history of gambling

Long before there were Dean Martin, martinis, and casinos shaped like New York City, there was gambling. Dice are thought to be the oldest gaming device. They were found in Sumerian royal tombs of Ur, which date back 3,000 years. And gamblers attracted to the pyramid-shaped Luxor Hotel and Casino in Las Vegas may be pleased to learn that dice also were found in the Great Pyramid of Cheops.

In Asia, the Chinese played wei-ch'i—a game with hundreds of pieces used to simulate war strategies—as early as 2300 B.C. And while no tip sheets have been found in Hindu temples, there's evidence that Indians bet on chariot races by 1500 B.C. The winners took home estates, slaves, and wives as well as money. Talk about comps!

Playing cards have only been around since the fourteenth century, but lotteries have been around for millennia. They weren't always used to raise money for state school systems and beneficial social programs, though. The ancient Aztecs used lotteries to determine the lucky lads and lasses who would have their still-beating hearts torn from their bodies to honor "benevolent" gods.

Ancient Romans loved all types of gambling. Don't forget, the Bible indicates that Roman guards at Golgotha cast lots for Jesus' personal belongings. Still, gambling was officially frowned upon in the enlightened empire of Rome. Just like today, laws made gambling illegal, but those edicts may not have always been strictly enforced.

In truth, throughout history, the pious and pinch-lipped have looked at gamblers askance. When the Catholic Church held sway over most of Europe, gaming was considered a close consort of most of the seven deadly sins, especially that rascal avarice. But gambling continued, despite—or perhaps because of—all that omnipresent piety. Let's face it—it's always been more fun to do something when you know you're not supposed to do it.

And let's not forget the New World. Early explorers found Native Americans playing games of chance. America's original Sin City, New Orleans, became the country's first major gambling center. In 1718, taverns and coffeehouses offered lodging and games of chance, until laws prohibiting gambling were passed in 1811. But people didn't stop rolling them bones, of course—gambling just went underground. In 1823, New Orleans's leaders decided they couldn't beat 'em. So they joined 'em, legalizing games and using profits to pay for schools and hospitals. Eventually, gambling was made illegal again in the Big Easy. Until, once again, it was legalized. The more things change . . .

Chicago also was a hot nineteenth century gambling Mecca, and of course, people who were experts at hiding a fifth and sixth ace up their sleeves were the ones to win the Wild West. Boot Hills are filled with folks who weren't very good cheaters.

In 1905, the wildest west town of them all was born: Las Vegas. In 1931, the state legislature legalized gambling, and soon, small casinos sprang up around the train depot where the city began. By the 1940s, some casinos were way out of town, on the highway that led to Los Angeles. Then, in 1946, mobster Benjamin "Bugsy" Siegel opened the fabulous Flamingo on what later would be christened the Strip. Bugsy helped transform Las Vegas from a town filled with sawdust joints and modern-day cowpokes to the glamorous city of sin it is today.

As Las Vegas's popularity grew, other communities, beginning with Atlantic City, decided they wanted a piece of the action. In years since, American Indian tribes have also won the right again to offer games of chance, and all but two states of the union offer gambling in one form or another.

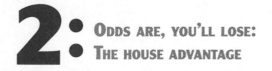

2: ODDS ARE, YOU'LL LOSE: THE HOUSE ADVANTAGE

You don't think those gleaming pleasure palaces called casinos make enough money to offer Monets and dancing minotaurs by giving money away, right? Get real. All games of chance are based on odds: the mathematical calculation of a given outcome's likelihood. And you can bet your life—really, it's that certain—that the casino, or house, will have the best odds for every game.

A simple way to think about odds is to take out a coin. If you flip it into the air, odds are one in two that the coin will land heads up. They're also one in two that tails will come up instead. There are only two sides to a coin, so there are only two possible outcomes. Simple, right? Even if you took that coin, tossed it 25 times, and it always came up heads, that's just a fluke. The odds are still 50/50 that the next time you throw George Washington into the air, he'll land on his tail.

Of course, casino games are more complicated. Once you've figured out the number of possible outcomes, you can figure out the probability, or odds, of getting a particular outcome. Look at your odds of winning if you wager the dice will come up "any craps"—meaning a two, three, or twelve. There's only one way to roll a two or twelve and two ways to roll a three. That means you determine probability by dividing four (the number of "any craps" combinations) by thirty-six (the possible number of combinations from two dice). The result, expressed as a percentage, is 11 percent.

Naturally, casinos don't offer simple games like bet on the coin toss. Instead, they favor games with a great probability of outcomes and variable odds. The one thing all games in a casino have in common is that their odds ultimately favor the house.

When you're at the casino, you might hit a winning streak—just like you might get heads twenty-five times—but odds are that over time the house will win back the money you've bet and then some. This is called the "house advantage." And it's the reason folks who make a killing on the tables are offered "comps," free stuff designed to get you to come back to the casino: meals, rooms, show tickets.

Casino managers are not being benevolent. They're betting that, if you come back, your hot streak will have cooled, and you'll pay back every penny you've earned from the casino. None of this is meant to imply that you should avoid gambling, because it can be a fun pastime. And odds don't take into account the great leveler: God-given, double-eyes-blind luck. It's just a word to the wise, guy.

3: TRICKS AND TRAPS: CASINO PSYCHOLOGY

Any casino is designed to be a jangling, jingling, show-girl-jiggling sensory overload. The word "sedate" will never be used to describe one. All these bells, whistles, and cocktail waitresses in various states of undress have a purpose: to separate you, the gambler, from your money. Casinos . . . God bless 'em.

The most ubiquitous games of chance in average casinos are slot machines, and casinos make excellent use of them.

When someone wins, alarms ring and coins fall with a thunderous crash into a metal basin designed to be as loud as possible. The bigger the win, the more sustained the alarm. If those sounds don't make you salivate as you dip eagerly into your pocket and seek the nearest slot machine, then you've obviously never heard of Pavlov and his amazing canines.

The casino's money-parting psychology is evident at the blackjack and craps tables as well. Slots are one of the few games that take real money. At table games, crisp fives and tens become stacks of colorful plastic. Dealers call them "nickels" and "dimes," so who cares if you lose them all. They're not real money, right?

Though all casino psychology is ultimately designed to make you eager to grab a roll of quarters or a stack of chips, psychology isn't just relegated to the games themselves. It actually affects the time-space continuum, because clocks are never visible in casinos, unless you look behind the workers inside the casino "cages" where winnings are gathered. You won't even know if it's day or night. Windows are scarce as royal flushes in most casinos. Is there a flash flood outside, turning the Strip into a roiling river? Who cares! Just fork over another stack of "nickels."

Casinos offer more than games of chance. Some have majestic towers from which you can catch once-in-a-lifetime views. Others feature free circus acts or wax museums. All have buffets, many offering all you can eat at very low prices. Casinos are also famous for their shows, ranging from no-name lounge acts to Hollywood has-beens to hot stars.

What do all of these diversions have in common? You can't get to them without first parting a Red Sea through rows of table games and slot machines. At the craps table, you'll hear excited shouts. And odds are, at least a few of those slot players are sitting calmly smoking a cigarette as alarms buzz over their heads and coins cascade into metal bins with thunderous crashes. It's not surprising that losing is silent in casinos, while winning is louder than a seven-nation army.

4: Sure fire, my butt: Don't trust sure-fire gambling strategies

Everyone knows these old adages: A fool and his money are soon parted. Anything that sounds too good to be true IS too good to be true. The difference with gambling is that you CAN get something for almost nothing, and though your odds of winning ten hands of blackjack in a row aren't very strong, it COULD happen. But remember one very important rule: Casinos offer games of skill and games of chance. There are no sure-fire strategies for games of chance, the results of which are purely random. The only thing that will cause you to win them is dumb luck.

In a typical casino, games of chance are the wheel of fortune, baccarat, craps, roulette, sic bo, slot machines, keno, bingo, casino war, and three-card poker. Even casual and first-time gamblers can easily see there's no sure-fire way to win a bet on the wheel of fortune. You pick a dollar amount, watch the casino employee give the wheel a spin, and then wait to see what happens. At some sawdust carnivals a carny can fix the wheel so that players never win a bet. But casino wheels aren't rigged, and no strategy will change physics—period.

Even though it's clear that games of chance live up to their name, novice gamblers can be tempted to believe that there are ways to guarantee wins at the craps, roulette, or baccarat table. These popular and sophisticated games don't have the carnival taint of a wheel of fortune. It's not so obvious these are games of chance, but they are. If you ever find an Internet site promising you big wins at the craps table if you'll just buy the site's handy dandy secrets of the known craps universe, don't bite. Finally, there are some gambling strategies that don't tell you how to win, they tell you how not to lose as much. But even these strategies are flawed and should be avoided.

One of the most well-known gambling systems is the Martingale System, also known as Double Up. It suggests you double your bet every time you lose because eventually you'll win. And when you do, the system suggests, you'll more than make up for what you've lost. But it doesn't always work. First of all, the Martingale System depends on one of gambling's most basic no-no's: Never chase your losses. When you're on a losing streak, quit once you reach your gambling limit. If you decide to go over your limit, certain that lady luck eventually will smile upon you, know that she usually remains aloof, and you're going to lose money. A lot of money. My-spouse-will-kill-me-or-at-the-very-least-divorce-me amounts of money. And that suggests another of the problems with the Martingale System. If you keep chasing your losses, you may get to a point where you can't double your bet because it exceeds the table limit.

The best gambling strategies won't guarantee that you win or lose, but they'll keep you from having to pawn your wedding ring. First of all, know how to play a game before you wager any money on it. Also, pick a gambling limit and stick to it. If you're a low-stakes player, then you may decide that $200 is the magic number. Once you lose that—even if it's only the second day of your vacation—then stay away from the tables. And finally, the time to raise your bet is when you're winning. NEVER raise your bet when you're losing. Odds are in the casino's favor, so don't throw good money after bad. Casinos make a lot of money from novice gamblers trying to turn around a losing streak.

5: The gambling superhighway: A primer on online gambling

No matter how much you read up on casino games, it can still be daunting to play them for the first time. At a casino, you'll find a lot of games that are confusing. You'll swear all the other players at the table are cool and collected and know exactly what they're doing. They're pros, you'll think, and you're a total novice. It's not a good feeling.

But don't worry. Casinos are filled with players who only look at ease. And thanks to the Internet, you can be more prepared than ever when you walk into a casino. The Internet is filled with information about everything—including gambling. There are a number of sites that allow you to play casino games, either for free or for the chance to win money. The advantages are several. You don't have to worry about looking foolish or adopting a poker face. You can walk yourself through a game until you're thoroughly familiar with it. You can even play naked . . . something not recommended at even the seediest Las Vegas casino.

Reputable online casinos offer a play-for-free option, which allows you to download your favorite game and learn to play it at your leisure. Make sure you play free before you hand over your credit card information, because you don't want mistakes to cost you anything. Free tutorials often include simulations of real casino play—the sound of tumbling dice, the scratching of cards on a table, applause for a winning hand, the sound of drunk guys trying desperately to pick up keno runners. Okay, that last one's not on there—at least not yet.

If you decide to try an online casino, you'll notice most of them are based in the Caribbean, Europe, or the Pacific Rim. Individual states and the federal government are trying to limit American-based online gambling sites. Since the passage of the Patriot Act, the pressure on American gambling sites has become even greater, due to fears that some sites are money-laundering operations for terrorist groups. If you're playing for money, it's best to check with your state to find out what laws apply to online gambling. If all of these political and legal issues make you nervous, then just confine yourself to the online casino's play-for-free option. And if a site doesn't allow you to download its gaming software without first offering a lot of personal information, then don't use that site.

Bricks-and-mortar casinos offer comps—free stuff for playing outrageous amounts of money at the tables—and online casinos offer bonuses. When you first sign up to play for money, you'll get a list of terms and conditions. Although it's tempting to skip all the fine print, you're better off skimming through it because it contains information about bonuses and play-throughs.

Online casinos offer varying bonuses for the amount of money you choose to wager. If you decide to authorize the casino to take $100 from your credit card, the likely bonus is around $25. Casinos typically cap their bonuses at $100, and all require a play-through before you can claim bonus money. A play-through means you can't withdraw your winnings until you've played a certain amount of money. Otherwise, folks would sign up, receive their bonuses, and then just take the money and run.

Play-throughs vary among sites, but they're generally ten times your original deposit, plus the bonus. So, if you wager $100 and get a $25 bonus, you've got to play up to $1,250 before you can withdraw anything. It sounds like a lot, but you'll be surprised how quickly you can wager that much. The fine print also lets you know what games are exempt from bonuses, so that's another reason to read it carefully.

If you can't easily find the terms and conditions for an online casino, then go to another one. You should also make sure the online casino offers good customer service, in the event of a computer glitch or in case you have questions. Sometimes there's a phone number offered on the site. Call it. See if you get a real, live person to help you. Many sites also offer real-time support in chat mode. This allows you to fire off your question, and have it answered immediately onscreen. If it's not easy to get help on a site, then don't commit money to it.

6: ONLINE SUCKER BETS: PROTECTING YOURSELF FROM INTERNET SCAMS

Ah, capitalism. It creates competition, which is good. And it creates crooked schemes and scams, which aren't. There are people—most likely teenage boys with poor social skills—who could start World War III any second because they can hack into practically any server. And there are folks who are so good at creating graphics they can easily appear to be legitimate online casinos. But the same technology that creates on-the-level online casinos can also create casinos designed simply to separate you from your money. So it's important to follow certain common-sense rules to ensure you're not scammed.

Make sure the online casino you consider uses a secure server. In most Windows-based programs, a little dialogue box will appear that contains a padlock on it, which informs you that you're about to enter a secure server. A secure server uses encryption software that scrambles your personal information as it's sent through cyberspace. The information is decoded only after it arrives at the secure server. If an online casino doesn't use a secure server, then at best it's a two-bit outfit and at worst it's trying to part you from your money.

Also beware of receiving e-mails from an Internet company that requests your credit, banking, or other personal information. Internet scam artists can create surprisingly legitimate-looking requests for your cash. Call the company that's supposedly sending you the request and ask if it actually has sent out the query. If the company doesn't know what you're talking about, then describe the e-mail you've received to a customer-service representative and ask him or her to report the scam to the powers that be.

You can also protect yourself by surfing through a few different casino sites. If you find that most of them offer, say, a $25 bonus for wagering $100, then you find one that claims to give $75 for that $100—it's probably not legit. Make sure you read the fine print if you think an online casino is making a claim that sounds too good to be true. It may turn out that you only get that $75 if there's a blue moon, you're playing between 3:30 A.M. and 3:31 A.M., and it's the sixth Sunday in November. As with anything in life: If it sounds too good to be true, then it's too good to be true. And you CAN bet on that.

One final way to protect yourself from Internet scams is to get a new credit card with a small balance and use it solely for online gambling. If the limit is $500, then you won't get taken to the cleaners if the casino is dishonest.

7: Take it to the limit: Set—and stick with—a gambling limit

The inner dialogue of many gamblers probably sounds a lot like this: "Oh man, it's Vegas baby! I know I said I was only gonna play with $500, but that was before I got here and started having all this fun. Dude, there's like free drinks—but only if I'm playing. Screw that limit. Where's the ATM? Sure, I've been losing and all, but lady luck will start smiling on me any minute. I won't tell my wife. She'd kill me. But once Irish eyes are smiling, I'll win so much cash, she won't be complaining then!"

Casinos love guys like this. That's why they offer them comps. That way, even if luck does turn out to be a lady, that sap will be back the next day, ready to flirt with her again. And eventually, the house will win because the odds are in its favor.

Casinos are designed to make players chase their losses. They reward winners, and you, of course, are a sophisticated card shark, a connoisseur of craps, a sultan of slots. And you'll prove it, even if you have to get a second or third mortgage! It's tempting to try to impress folks in a casino. Take the dealer, for instance. Like the famous Beefeater guards of England, they are often an impassive lot. Those inscrutable faces can entice novice players into making a bold, daring move that will raise an eyebrow or earn a smile.

And if you're a guy, then you certainly don't want to look like a loser in front of a beautiful woman. That's why some casinos pay attractive women to be at gaming tables. If she compliments you on your play, then you'll probably keep playing, and think, "The light bill? Aw, hell. The kids can do their homework on slates with charcoal by the light of the fire. It worked for Abraham Lincoln, and he became president!" You may even decide to impress yourself. You've got a coworker who's always getting promoted because of his daring? Well, you're more daring than that chump! Just wait until you get back to the office and brag about how your nerves of steel earned you enough dough-re-mi to take a six-month vacation!

Casinos make it easy to gamble. If you've just gotten out of a taxi after a ten-hour flight, then the sounds of winners can be hard to ignore as you register for your room. Jet lag? You're too much of a man for that. Naps are for wimps and infants. Let's get started. Viva Las Vegas! Casinos gamble on guests wanting to make wagers the moment they walk in the door, and they usually win that bet. You don't expect a kid in a candy store to peruse each shelf and jar carefully before making her selection, now do you? But the fact remains: The time to gamble is when you're rested and in full control of your faculties.

The best way to avoid the chorus of siren songs that lure you away from your money is to set a gambling limit before you walk through the casino's door. Don't bet more than you can afford to lose . . . And that's true if the loss is monetary or emotional. Some folks can afford to lose five grand, but if dropping that makes them feel like losing scum, then the emotional toll isn't worth the risk for them. Your best bet, if you're going to be at a casino for several days, is to decide on a daily bankroll. Take only the chosen amount with you to the tables or slot machines.

And finally, play to win. Don't think by being a cynical, too-cool-to-fool sort that you'll come out feeling like a winner. If you go into a casino thinking, I'm bringing $500 to lose, then you're playing not to lose, instead of playing to win. You'll make bets because you've got a what-the-hell kind of attitude. You'll make a large bet just to be able to say you did it, thinking you're going to lose $500 anyway, right? If you're playing smart, playing to win, then you're a lot more likely to walk out a winner than a preordained loser.

8: A FOOL AND HIS MONEY: DON'T PLAY IF YOU DON'T UNDERSTAND

Casinos are theme parks for adults. They're filled with excitement and fast-paced action, the chance to win something for almost nothing, and even free drinks. The shouts of winners are like the screams of delight from kids riding down Splash Mountain. And the theme park illusion is even greater from the outside of a casino. Disney parks have Cinderella's castle. Las Vegas has the Excalibur—based on that same castle. Amusement parks have roller coasters. Well, so does the New York–New York Hotel and Casino.

The problem with being lulled into the tingling excitement of childhood when you're an adult in Sin City is that casino fun requires some advance knowledge, unlike theme parks. At theme parks, you simply find a ride, wait in line for a really long time, and go. But you need to know how to play casino games. If you walk up to a table and you're ignorant, then you're going to lose money, and it doesn't take long to lose a lot. It's no fun to lose—at anything—and it's especially galling to lose hard-earned money.

Slot machines are popular because they're so simple. But even they require some understanding. Ask yourself these questions: How many coins does the machine take for a maximum payout? Does the machine have bonus payouts? Have you enrolled in the casino's slot club? And most importantly, ask yourself: Did you get your free slot player's glove? Yes, some casinos have these. They're designed either to keep you from picking up germs or to keep you from getting blisters as you pull the handles on your favorite machines. Hey, this is Vegas. You should get any free thing that's coming to you, no matter how dopey it sounds.

Table games can be extremely complicated. Throwing caution to the winds and laying your money down without understanding the finer points of a game is not smart. Just because you've played blackjack with your buddies for beer money doesn't mean you should head straight to the tables. For example, the rules on when the dealer must take a hit can differ from casino to casino. Plus, your odds of winning are better at a single-deck table than at one with a five-deck shoe.

There are at least three different ways to make sure you know what you're doing at all games before you make your first wager. Consult a book like this one or find one that's designed specifically for the game that interests you most before you leave home.

As explained in number 6, online casinos also offer a chance to play games of chance on your own and with the safety of not wagering real money. Almost all Internet casinos offer a play-for-free option that gives you the chance to learn the peccadilloes of various games. And finally, you can learn how to play a casino's games at the casino itself. All of them offer tutorials on individual table games. Though you may feel like a lightweight stepping up to a table to get the skinny on the world of craps, you'd feel like a total idiot if you played without an understanding of the game and then lost your savings. In "real life," most people approach new ventures with a healthy dose of skepticism and caution. Casinos employ an arsenal of psychological tricks and traps to lure you into throwing caution out the window—if you can find a window in the casino, that is. Arm yourself with knowledge, then a strip of casinos really can become the happiest place on earth.

9: MAKING PROGRESS:
PROGRESSIVE MONEY-MANAGEMENT STRATEGIES

Gambling experts are full of advice about how to protect your bankroll—the amount of money you've brought with you to gamble. Some argue you should play as though your winnings didn't belong to you. The thinking goes: It's the casino's money, right? You came in with $500. That $200 you won is cream. Others say that's dumb. Once you win money, it's *your* money. Pretending it isn't could cause you to play recklessly. Some say that when you win big, you should let that bet ride one last time. Others say that's crazy. Knowing when—and being able—to walk away from the table when you're ahead is one of gambling's golden rules. There's no way to guarantee you'll walk away a winner from any casino.

Bankroll management is all about minimizing losses. What follows are some ways to ensure you have fun gambling and then leave—if not a winner—then at least without a scarlet letter "L" on your forehead.

- **Build your bankroll into your travel plans.** If you've saved up a few thousand dollars to spend on hotels, restaurants, and nongambling activities, then treat that money like it doesn't exist when you get to the gaming tables.

- **Treat your bankroll as money expressly to be used for gambling.** Don't think to yourself: "I'm going to lose this cash." But don't start expecting to double it and pay for your oldest daughter's orthodontia either. Be able to answer with an honest "no" the question: Will I lose several nights of sleep if I lose this bankroll?

- **Remember that comps are a casino's way of keeping winners on a leash.** Casino officials are quite adept at sniffing out high-roller wannabes from packs of neophytes dreaming of getting "free" stuff. If you're a low-stakes player, don't throw your money into the toilet just so you can get a free ticket to a Donnie & Marie tribute show in the Feelin' Lucky Showroom.

- **Protect your money by taking breaks.** If you win a particularly big pot, then quit while you're ahead. Walk away a winner. There . . . Isn't that intoxicating? You are a playa. You can hold your head up high. The odds favor the house in every single game, so you will lose if you keep playing. But if you win and take a break, then you can decide—calmly and not in the heat of the moment—whether to continue gambling.

- **Wear a watch, and keep an eye on the time.** Casinos do their best to create sensory-manipulation chambers. Quit every hour or so and walk around until your head is clear. Go to the arcade and play a game that can only earn you bragging rights and the chance to put your name on the high-score list.

• **Quit after a certain number of hands or slot pulls, no matter what.** This is a good strategy if you don't want to be a slave to time.

Whatever strategy you prefer, you need to find a way to pull yourself out of the lull a casino's bells, whistles, bright lights, and ecstatic shouts create. A good rule of thumb is to gamble only as long as it makes you happy. If you get on a losing streak and start raising your bets to get your money back, odds are you'll just lose more. And then you'll feel downright miserable.

Gambling can be like trying unsuccessfully to lose weight. After a week of exercise and eating rabbit food, you get on the scale and . . . well, come and kiss my great Aunt Fanny. You've actually gained two pounds. The most natural reaction at this time is: Forget this. It's not worth it. Double bacon cheeseburger and enormous-sized fries, here I come! Sometimes a losing streak can evoke that same crazy bravado. However, unlike dieting, you probably won't notice your arteries clogging right away. You will, however, notice that your bankroll is gone and so is most of your travel money. And your children's college fund. And your church tithe. The single most important gambling rule is never, never, never chase losses with larger bets. Let gambling be fun and exciting, not something that makes you consider hari-kari.

10: STICK WITH 50:50 PERCENT GAINS OR LOSSES ARE YOUR FRIENDS

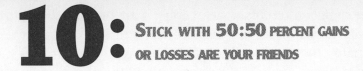

Let's face it . . . a lot of money-management tips are hard to remember, especially in the heat of battle. You may stock up on strategies before you get to the airport and commit them to memory. But it's a lot like cramming for a test the night before you take it. You'll remember bits and pieces of the information, but you may not be able to extract the right piece knowledge at the right time.

So, here's a simple strategy. Quit gambling when you've doubled or halved your bankroll for each game. Gather at least an outline of what you want to play and how much you want to devote to each game. If you're afraid the craps tables'll intimidate you, but you want to play, then plan to devote just a sliver of your bankroll to the game. Of course, you don't have to put yourself in a straitjacket. You may roll them bones and decide it's the coolest game you've ever played. But if you decide to wager more on the craps tables, then plan to wager less on another game.

Whatever you do, keep your overall bankroll the same, no matter how you decide to divide it. And then play the games you like as much as you like—until you've won or lost 50 percent of that original bankroll. Just count the bankroll

. . . not what you win from the house. If you come in with $200 to spend on the blackjack tables, for example, then play until you've won $300, or you're reduced to $100. Then walk away. Later that day or the following day, if you go back to blackjack, then play the $300 like it's $200. Put that extra hundred bucks in your pocket. If you weren't so lucky, play the $100 like it's $100 because that's what's left of your original bankroll. Play until you've gotten to $300 or you're down to $50.

Keep going that way. If you double your money during at least one session of play, then the most you'll lose is $100. If you come out ahead a few times, then you're a winner. If you lose every day, then at least you've only lost $200, the amount you decided in advance you could lose if lady luck smiled elsewhere. It's a simple strategy, but if you stick to it, gambling will be fun, win or lose. Always remember: If gambling ceases to be fun, then cease gambling!

PART 2:

TURNS OF FRIENDLY CARDS:
CARD GAMES

POKER HAS BECOME ANOTHER OF AMERICA'S PASTIMES, though there is something sort of strange about watching celebrities and professionals playing poker on TV, the way you'd watch a baseball game. What's next—celebrity Scrabble? Nevertheless, poker's popularity as a spectator sport is proof that it's an intriguing game, about equal parts skill, luck, and acting.

In this part of the book, you'll first learn a bit of poker's history, including jaunts into the Wild West and some time spent rollin' on the river, on paddle-wheel steamers. We'll learn the basics of the game's most popular varieties, before turning to strategies that may help you walk away a winner from the table. You'll find out what you can learn from different betting rounds, how to win against different types of opponents, and how to keep others guessing, so you'll have a better chance to win their money.

And even though it may seem like stud poker is the only card game available in a casino, it's nowhere near the only kind of poker you can play. Some varieties, like Caribbean Stud, Pai Gow, and Let It Ride, are played against the house rather than against other players. These can be a good way to get your feet wet before wading in with the sharks at a Texas Hold 'Em table.

Then you'll learn more about that other casino favorite, blackjack, which offers the lowest house advantage of any casino game. Blackjack remains a popular casino staple because it's challenging, but not so challenging that newcomers can't quickly grasp the game's basics. You'll learn some strategies for maximizing your chances of winning and also why blackjack insurance should be avoided.

Finally, you'll learn about baccarat, a game growing in popularity as casinos introduce scaled-down versions with low table limits. The game probably attracts more high rollers than any other in the average casino. But despite its aura of glitz, glamour, sophistication, and wealth, baccarat is pretty easy to play and doesn't have to deprive you of your children's inheritance.

11: GIVE ME A HAND: THE HISTORY OF POKER

Poker has become very popular, with celebrity tournaments popping up on practically every cable channel. The game is exciting because it offers gamblers a level playing field. Players compete against each other, and he or she with the most skill wins. You don't even need a winning hand to collect the pot of money bet during each hand. You just need the ability to keep a poker face when bluffing.

The origins of poker are unclear, but most experts agree that it began around the turn of the nineteenth century in New Orleans, home of the famous French Quarter and an early gambling haven. The word "poker" is believed to be an Americanization of the French name for the game, "poque."

In the 1820s, the game was played using a twenty-card deck with four aces, kings, queens, jacks, and tens. There were no suits, and hands were ranked from one pair to fulls, or full houses. The standard fifty-two-card decks appeared in the 1850s. The modern deck offers a more varied game and allows more than four people to play at a time. By the 1870s, poker had basically developed into its present form, although there were some early disagreements, such as: Does a flush beat a straight, or does a straight beat a flush?

Ultimately, the flush won out. But don't you wonder how many folks wound up in Boot Hill over that silly disagreement?

With the exception of a form called Lowball, there are fundamental similarities among competitive poker varieties. The hand rank is the same, and in each, hands are comprised of five cards. Before getting into more complex card-playing strategy, here's a quick round up of how the different hands rank:

- The manna of poker is the royal flush: ace, king, queen, jack, and ten of the same suit.
- Next best is the straight flush: five sequential, lower cards of the same suit.
- Then there's four-of-a-kind, exactly what its name suggests: four cards of the same rank.
- A full house is three-of-a-kind and a pair.
- A flush is five nonsequential cards of the same suit.
- A straight is five sequential cards of different suits.
- Three-of-a-kind has three cards of the same rank.
- Two pair is two sets of pairs, and it beats one pair, only two cards of the same rank.
- The lowest hand in poker is one that has none of these combinations, also called a "crap hand"—or worse.

12: NOT QUITE 57 VARIETIES: POKER'S BASIC FACES AND HOW TO PLAY THEM

For each variety of poker the object is the same—to win the pot. You can win two ways: by having the highest hand or by making the other players believe you have the highest hand—known as bluffing. Bluffing is risky business—to do it, you have to bet enough money so that other players will throw in, or fold, their cards before the end of the round. If you're bluffing, it means you're increasing the bet while holding a lousy hand. But hey, this is gambling! It's not successful if it doesn't make you sweat bullets.

In all poker games, someone must deal out the cards. In casinos, the house always has a dealer. The dealer plays and bets last, which gives him an advantage during the play of some poker varieties. In other varieties, even though the casino's dealer always does the shuffling and dealing, a button is passed around to the individual players. If a player has the button, then she plays and bets last.

Poker games also contain an ante, a small bet made prior to the first betting round. Betting rounds vary, depending on whether you're playing a stud game like Seven-Card Stud or Texas Hold 'Em, or whether you're playing a draw poker game. (Each type will be discussed soon enough in the points to come.)

Finally, each type of poker played in a casino contains a rake, a portion of all bets the house takes after each round.

Seven-Card Stud is the most popular form of stud poker. "Stud" refers to the play, not the players. In stud games, some cards are face-up, while others are face-down. In Seven-Card Stud, the game begins with an ante, usually 10 percent of the minimum bet. Let's assume you're playing on a $5 to $10 table. The ante would be 50 cents. There are five rounds of betting in Seven-Card Stud.

For the first round—called third street—two cards are dealt face-down and the third face-up. The low card opens. The low card bettor can start with a $1 bet, which can be raised by $4. After that, raises for that round will be in $5 increments. To stay in the game, you must call—or throw in at least the minimum bet during each round. You can also raise the bet by an increment of $5. Or you can fold during any round.

Round two is called fourth street because players still in the game are dealt a fourth card, face-up. Beginning with this round, all bets have to be in $5 increments. Round three is called fifth street, and you receive another card dealt face-up during it. Round four is sixth street. Players still in the game get another face-up card. The final round ends with a showdown. After bets and raises are made, remaining players put together the best hand they can with five out of seven cards. The player with the highest-ranking hand is the winner and gets all the chips.

Texas Hold 'Em, or simply Hold 'Em, has become a popular form of player-against-player poker, especially in Las Vegas and on television. As in Seven-Card Stud, the house's dealer always deals the cards. But a button is placed in front of a player from round to round. The player with the button is the imaginary dealer. The player to her left makes the first bet. It's advantageous to be the dealer because you bet last, so you can get the lay of the land from how your opponents bet.

If you're to the left of the button-holding imaginary dealer, then you have to make what's called a blind bet on the first round. The dealer deals two cards face-down to each player during the first round. The first bettor then must make an opening bet, which cannot be lower than the table minimum. For a $5 to $10 table, for example, a $1 or $2 bet is fine. Other players can raise that $4 or sometimes $5. Thereafter, in the low rounds of betting, bets must be at least $5.

After the first bets are made, the dealer turns over three cards on the board face-up—these cards are called the flop for some reason. They're also called community cards because every player will use them to supplement his or her two-card hand. Once the dealer turns over three cards, betting continues. Again, you can play or fold, but to play, you must put in the minimum bet and the raised bet, if there is one. For the next round, the dealer turns over a fourth community card, which begins the high round. At this point, your minimum bet must be the upper limit of the table's minimum. For the final round, a fifth card is placed face-up on the table.

Players still in the game make their bets, and then it's time for the showdown. The hands must include your two face-down cards and three of the upturned cards. The highest hand wins the pot.

Jacks or Better is the most popular form of draw poker. Draw poker is so called because, during the course of each hand, you can discard up to five of the five cards you are dealt and draw new ones. Draw poker is a closed variation of the game, meaning that all of a player's cards are unseen by other players. There are only two betting rounds in Jacks of Better. The dealer always deals the cards, but a button placed in front of a player makes him the imaginary dealer.

For round one, players are dealt five cards face-down. The first player to the left of the imaginary dealer who has at least a pair of jacks or better can start off the betting. Players who don't at least have jacks or better must check, or pass on the opportunity to bet. After a bet is made, subsequent players can place the minimum bet or higher, raise the initial bet, or fold.

Players in the second round can place up to five cards face-down on the table, which lets the dealer know you want that many new cards. The player closest to the imaginary dealer's left starts the betting. The highest hands win.

For the most part, winning hands in draw poker are the same as those in the stud games. But all bets are off for Lowball, because the low hand wins. The best hand you can get in Lowball—called the wheel or bicycle—is an ace, two, three, four, and five. They don't have to be of the same suit. What's important is the worth—or lack thereof—of your hand's face value. In Lowball, an ace counts as one.

The game begins with the dealer handing out five cards. After that, the player to the left of the imaginary dealer must bet at least the table minimum. No one can check in the first round of Lowball. Based on your hand, you can bet, raise, or fold in the first round. The remaining players in the second and final betting round can exchange up to four cards for new ones. Players bet or fold. The lowest hand wins.

13: I'VE GOT MY EYE ON YOU: THE IMPORTANCE OF PEERING AT OTHER PLAYERS' PECCADILLOES

One key to winning at poker is remembering that you're playing against human beings, not robots. In daily life, you've probably become adept at reading body language and sizing up people based on behavior. Use the same skills when you sit down at casino poker tables.

Take the "loose player" type, for instance. This is the guy who's out for action. He loves to play. He'll go all the way to the final betting round, no matter what he has. Sometimes he wins because of his aggressive style. But he's actually pretty easy to beat. You can't bluff a loose player, so don't even try. He loves the competition so much that he won't care if you have a great hand or just smoke and mirrors. You'll get the edge over a loose player if you play a fundamental, no-frills game in the early rounds. Bet when you have a good hand, don't when you don't. During the showdowns of later rounds, though, start calling more often because loose players tend to stay in the game with weaker hands.

The "tight player" is the opposite of the loose player. Slow and steady, she makes and calls bets only when she's got a good hand. If she calls, she means business. But she's still beatable. Don't call her bets as often because you can trust her to make them only when she believes she's got the goods. If you have a strong hand, go ahead and call her bets. If she raises, then think carefully. Don't call automatically. Assume she's got a very good hand, and only call if the strength of your hand justifies it.

Some players like to bluff—a lot. Call their bets frequently if you have any sort of hand. Once you've determined that someone is a frequent bluffer, then you know you're pretty safe keeping the pot going. Also, if someone likes to bluff, then call him for at least a few rounds in case you're able to build your hand from nothing to something. And if you have a *really* strong hand, pray that your opponent is a congenital bluffer, because you'll win with a good hand every time.

There are those players who never bluff, but they are also your friends, because they're very predictable. If one of these players has a bad hand, he'll fold. You're best off folding marginal calls against this type of player. Call less often with a questionable hand, and don't get bluffed out by any high cards the nonbluffer may show.

14: Wanna make a bet? Use your bet to gain valuable knowledge

You can't learn anything about your fellow players until the betting rounds start. But once the chips start falling, you can learn plenty. This knowledge is the key to walking out of the poker hall flush with success, not busted into bankruptcy.

Poker is a game of infinite complexities—some luck, some skill, some psychology, some acting. But there really are very few moves to make during betting rounds. You either: call ("see" someone's bet, or bet the same amount as the previous bet), raise (put in more than the previous bet), fold (decide there's no hope for your hand and give up before you lose a lot of money), or—if no players before you have made a bet—you can check (stay in the game without betting). It's important to remember what it means for a player to raise. The implied message is, "I've got a good hand here, so stay in the game at your own risk. You have been warned." If someone raises, and you have a crap hand, then go out early unless you're sure the person who's raised is a congenital bluffer.

Most poker strategists will tell you there are actually three moves in poker: raising, checking, and folding. Calling, they say, is for total wusses. But sometimes calling can be beneficial. For example, you can determine if an opponent is a loose, aggressive player by calling. If you're playing Texas Hold 'Em, and the flop isn't particularly helpful—say a face card and two "babies" or low cards of different suits—but you're holding a strong pair, call with those who stay in the round. An aggressive player will likely raise the bet, in an effort to get you to fold or raise. If it's just two of you, then check. He'll probably raise. Then call. By this time, your opponent has probably figured out you're holding something good, but he's committed to the round. It should be clear what type of player he is by his next move. If aggressive, he'll keep going. If not, he'll fold. Either way, you're likely to come out a winner.

Bets give you a chance to observe opponents' play styles *and* their style of deception. How often, for instance, does an opponent try to conceal the strength of her hand? Half the time? Only one-fourth of the time? You'll find out by what she chooses to do during the betting round. Sometimes an opponent will raise even if all he's got is a pair of tens or a ten-jack of the same suit. You'll learn this once the betting rounds are complete. If that's his style of deception, then you can prevent it from working on you in future rounds of play.

Finally, a note of caution is required. At low-limit poker tables, other players are probably not paying much attention to their opponents' behavior. They're just playing because it's an exciting pastime, not to make a living. Figuring out what kind of players they are by how they bet is likely to work. But don't get overconfident. If you take the same psychology to a high-stakes game, it could backfire. Seasoned players will sniff you out immediately. Don't run with the big dogs until you've mastered the art of wrangling the puppies.

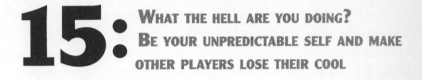

15: **What the hell are you doing?**
Be your unpredictable self and make
other players lose their cool

The most important thing to check at the poker table is your emotions, not your cards. Showing frustration at a run of bad luck or inordinate joy at a run of good luck can get you in trouble. So can playing consistently. Really good poker players evaluate your every move, and if they can figure you out, then you're toast—they'll eat you for breakfast. With that in mind, imagine how much pain and suffering you'll cause other players if you're impossible to read. But it takes firm control of your emotions—and some theatrical ability—to be successful with inconsistent play.

Take the bluff, for example. Some players bluff often, and some don't do it at all. Try mixing these styles. If you have a bad hand, bluff with gusto. Raise like there's no tomorrow. And if your bluff is successful, make a point of letting the other players see your cards. Gloat just a tiny bit. This will increase the chance of your opponents making a foolish move. Imagine the poor schlub who had the best hand, and then folded to your bluff. Most likely, she'll be rattled. She'll decide she'll be damned if you're going to do that to her again. But play it cool. Play a nice, conservative game until you have what you're certain will be a winning hand. Raise just like you did during that earlier bluffing session. Odds are, many players will decide you're just raising with rubbish—again. Great! Let them believe that. Then, when you throw down two bullets and three ladies (two aces, three queens), feel free to gloat just a bit once more as you rake in the chips.

Another way to affect your opponents' collective blood pressure is to play fast and loose with tight and loose play. Loose poker players love action. They are likely to stay in a round regardless of what cards they hold and regardless of bluffers. Tight players, on the other hand, play close to the vest, raising only when they have good hands and folding every time they don't. Once your opponents get a read on your style, you're handing them the keys to beating you. So, the solution is to flip-flop your play from time to time.

Flip-flopping play sounds easy in the abstract, but imagine doing this with six pairs of eyes boring holes into you and a portion of your money at stake. Remember: Keep your emotions in check. The pressure to play a consistent game can be enormous, simply because it feels safe. When you add angry opponents to that safety factor, then the pressure is increased exponentially. One way to counteract this pressure is to make it clear you're a beginner. Broadcast to other players: "Oh gee, I'm new at this. I don't know what I'm doing. Tee hee." Of course, veteran players don't have much patience for neophytes—although they should, since beginners are their bread and butter—but at least you won't have anyone suspecting that you, in fact, are playing inconsistently on purpose.

16: You've got to know when to hold em— oh, you know the rest: The art of folding

Everyone knows the famous Kenny Rogers song about a gambler who offers sage advice when it comes to knowing when to hold your cards and when to fold them. Beginning players may have a harder time maneuvering through this labyrinth of good moves versus really bad ones. But there are a few things to keep in mind to help you determine when to hold 'em—and call or raise 'em—and when to cut your losses.

First of all, consider card odds and pot odds. Card odds refer to the probability that you'll improve your hand with a draw or with the next round of dealing. If you have a pair among your first three cards, then your odds of improving your hand are between 2.5 to one and three to one—pretty good. Card odds for common hands are as follows: If you have an inside straight—say a three, five, six, seven—then your probability of picking up a four to complete it is eleven to one, or not very good. Your odds are a little better if you have an open-ended straight—say a three, four, five, six. You have about a one to five chance of picking up a two or seven. If you have four cards to a flush—say four spades—then your odds of picking up one more spade are four to one. If you have four cards to an inside straight flush, your odds of getting the card you need are three to one. If you've got four cards to an open-end straight flush, then your odds are about two to one.

You've also got to compare the card odds with the pot odds. Pot odds are the ratio of the amount of money you have to put in the pot compared to the value of the pot. If the pot is worth $500 and you have to put in $5 to continue playing, the pot odds are 100 to one. If you have to put in $50 to stay in the game, the pot odds are ten to one. In order to decide whether to stay in a particular round of poker, you need to determine both pot and card odds and make your best guess. If this sounds difficult, don't worry. Professional poker players weren't born with supercomputers in their fingertips. They've spent years at the tables determining pot odds. The best thing a novice can do is observe and learn from better players—preferably without going broke first.

Other ways to make the call, raise, or fold decision include the following:

- If you have a strong hand and believe you have the advantage over most of your opponents, then raise instead of calling.

- If you start out with weak cards, then fold. Don't cling to the hope that subsequent betting rounds will dramatically improve your situation.
- If you have a decent hand but one you believe your opponents can beat, fold too.
- If you get a top pair early on in a stud game, then raise unless it becomes clear another player has stepped into a giant pile of good luck.

In general, raising is better than calling when you have good cards. It's a way of determining what kind of opponents you're playing against.

17: I DID IT MY WAY: FIND YOUR OWN STYLE OF POKER PLAY

You have to be disciplined to win consistently at the poker table, and one building block of discipline is rules. Yes, you're in a casino, and you want to cling to the idea that anything goes. But that kind of thinking leads to mistakes. You play poker against opponents and not the house, so you'll get eaten alive if you're an undisciplined player.

The good news is that you can make your own rules at the poker table. You've just got to make sure you keep them, no matter how much pressure you face. Professional poker player and author Andy Nelson offers some of his own laws in *Poker: 101 Ways to Win.* These guidelines can serve as a template when you formulate your own personal poker code. For starters, always gamble with gambling money, not with the mortgage or that $50 you owe your best friend. Playing with such "committed" money is self-defeating because it keeps you from making correct choices at the table.

Never play when something away from the tables is affecting your mental state. If you've just had a big argument with your husband or wife, forget it. You're likely to make foolish choices when you're unsettled emotionally, and then when you lose, you're going to be even unhappier. For that matter, if you make a bonehead play and lose a hand, don't play while you're upset. Call a time out. Get away from the table. Otherwise, you'll throw more good money after bad. Remember: Always play with a self-imposed gambling limit. Play conservatively until you start to figure out other players' peccadilloes.

Discipline at poker also requires you to find the right style of play for you. If you find it impossible to keep a poker face when holding a killer hand, then you probably shouldn't try to bluff. If you're just naturally a loose player who enjoys staying with each round until it's all over, that's fine—if you're aware of it. If that style of play makes you happier than winning often, then you should enforce a lower limit on yourself.

If you feel more comfortable with tight play, then focus on keeping your emotions in check. Don't get rattled when conservative play causes you to lose a pot that could have been yours. Once you know the rules that work for you, then you can break them from time to time, if you realize it will be advantageous to do so. Deviating from disciplined, rule-centered play when deviation is warranted can make you a big winner. But not having a firm grasp on your own set of rules and your own style of play will definitely make you a loser.

18: You stud, you: How to play Caribbean Stud Poker

Pirates or manly Rastafarians did not invent this style of poker. But Caribbean Stud Poker does get its name from where it was invented: on cruise ships floating around—you guessed it—the Caribbean. And here's where the "stud" part comes in: The game is played like Seven-Card Stud Poker, with a mix of cards laid face-up and face-down on the table. Caribbean Stud is not poker in the traditional sense because it is played against the dealer, like blackjack. It's a very popular game in most casinos because it offers a progressive jackpot that can rise into the hundreds of thousands. It's exciting to watch the numbers in that jackpot spin out of control as you play. Of course, the reason the payoff keeps getting larger is because it's rarely won.

A Caribbean Stud Poker table resembles a blackjack table. The dealer stands in the center of a semicircle around which a number of players compete. The game is played with a single deck of cards, minus jokers. You begin the game by placing an ante bet. The minimum ante at most casinos is $5. The dealer then doles out five cards at a time face-down to each player. At most casinos, a device called a shuffle master spits out five cards at once. The dealer then deals herself four cards face-down, and the last card she deals herself is called the upcard because it's dealt face-up.

Players then pick up their cards and have to make a decision. Let's say the dealer's showing an ace or face card. You turn over your five cards and have nothing that remotely resembles a winning poker hand. You can't turn in any of your cards for new ones—you're stuck with what you've got. If your hand is just plain lousy, you can fold. But you lose your ante bet. If you decide to play, you have to wager a call bet. It must be at least double your ante bet. After all players have folded or offered their call bets, the dealer turns over her other four cards.

Winning hands in Caribbean Stud Poker are ranked the same as in regular poker. But there's one difference. The dealer's hand must "qualify," or the game ends. To qualify, she must have at least a king and an ace or better. If she doesn't, then you get even money on your ante bet. Your $5 becomes $10. Your call bet is a push, meaning you don't lose anything. But you don't win anything either. If the dealer has qualified, then her hand is compared with the players' hands. Let's say she's got two pair, threes and fives. You've got two pair, sevens and eights. You win! The call bonus typically is two to one for two pair. If you've got two pair, twos and fours, when the dealer has threes and fives, then you lose your ante and call bets. The amount you win, therefore, is based on two things: beating the dealer's hand and having a good hand yourself. The better the hand, the more you win.

Now, about that progressive jackpot. It's really a side bet and has nothing to do with whether you beat the dealer. The jackpot bet is usually $1, and you're not required to place it in order to play your hand. But you might as well. If you don't make the jackpot bet, then you won't be eligible for payouts from the progressive pool. At most casinos, you have to have a flush or higher to qualify for part of the jackpot. The breakdown is usually like this: flush, $75; full house, $100; four of a kind, $500; straight flush, 10 percent of the total jackpot; royal flush, 100 percent of the meter, which is often in the tens of thousands of dollars. That booty would make even the bloodthirstiest pirate of the Caribbean dance a jig and sing, "Yo, ho, ho and a bottle of rum."

19: HOW TO BE A PIRATE OF THE CARIBBEAN: STRATEGIES FOR CARIBBEAN STUD POKER

The house edge for Caribbean Stud Poker is about 5.2 percent on the ante bet, which is pretty high for a card game. It's high because the game can end before it begins if the dealer's hand doesn't qualify. But the odds are better on the combined ante and call bets. They drop to about 2.6 percent. Bottom line: The odds aren't great for this game. But it's easy to play, and there's that outside chance you'll get some of the progressive jackpot.

There's not much strategy in Caribbean Stud Poker. You're stuck with the hands you're dealt, so if they're lousy you'll be left crying in your pina colada. You can't bluff other players because you're playing against the dealer and not against them. But there are some strategies to remember that will increase your odds of winning.

Call with any pair or better, no matter how small. It's tempting to fold with a small pair, but remember that your job is to beat the dealer, who also must call if he has nothing more than a pair of deuces. The dealer will get a pair 42 percent of the time, on average. And if all YOU have is a pair of deuces, you still could beat the dealer if he's got nothing more than an ace and king high. Studies indicate that folding small pairs increases the house edge to about 7 percent. And if the dealer doesn't qualify, you'll at least get back your ante bet in case you have better luck next time.

Call if you have a busted straight: ace, king, queen, jack, and any card other than 10. This will beat a dealer's ace-king hand. The hand appears even stronger if the dealer shows as his upcard any card that's a pair for one of ours. It reduces his chance of having a pair. If you have a garbage hand, then fold and give up your ante bet. Just as it can be tempting to fold a small pair, it can also be tempting to play with a garbage hand, hoping the dealer won't qualify. The odds are against this being a successful strategy, so don't do it. Be patient. Even if you get five garbage hands in a row, don't start playing stupidly. Remember . . . you've got to know when to fold 'em, even if you're playing Caribbean Stud Poker.

As for the progressive jackpot, the best thing to do is find a casino with a very high jackpot. It's that simple. Why play your $1 wager for the chance to win $50,000 when your Washington could net you $200,000. And avoid tables where the progressive has just been hit. Go for greater progressives if you really want to be a stud at Caribbean Stud.

20: RIDE, RIDE, RIDE, WON'T YOU LET IT RIDE: HOW TO PLAY LET IT RIDE POKER

Let It Ride was created by the Shuffle Master Corporation and introduced in Nevada casinos in 1993. It's a variation of five-card poker, but you play against the house and not other players. It's different from traditional poker in two other ways as well: Your hand is a combination of the three cards you're dealt and the two cards held by the dealer. And Let It Ride is distinctive because of the feature that gives the game its name, which allows you to withdraw bets.

Let It Ride is played on a table similar to a blackjack table. The dealer is in the center of a semi-circle, with

players around the outside. Each player spot has three circles for a bet, labeled "1," "2," and "$." You must place the
minimum wager in each circle. Don't be too concerned if your
hand is god-awful because you can remove two of those bets.

Place your bets on the circle, and the dealer will give you
three cards face-down, shuffled and spit out in threes from
a device created by—naturally—the Shuffle Master Corporation. The dealer finishes by dealing herself two cards face-
down. At that point, it's time to look at your cards and play. If
your hand isn't very promising, you can remove the first bet.
Don't touch the chips, though. Scrape your three cards toward
you on the table, to let the dealer know you want to reclaim
bet number one. She will push your chip(s) toward you.

The dealer then turns over the first of her two "community
cards," so called because they're used by every player at the
table. You have the same decision as before. Let's say you took
back your first bet. Your hand is a two, three, and a ten. In Let
It Ride, payouts are made for any pair of tens or better. If the
dealer's first card is a ten, then you know you're going to win at
least even money during this game. But if the community card
and your cards are not promising, then you can scrape your
cards on the table and reclaim bet number two. You can remove
the second bet, even if you let the first bet ride.

The dealer then turns over her second card for the "showdown" round. It's a showdown because this is the one bet you
can't remove. Unlike traditional five-card draw poker, you're
stuck with these five cards—good, bad, or ugly. Once again, let's

say you've got a two, three, and a ten. The dealer's first over-turned card is a queen. That doesn't help you. But her second card is a ten. Score! If you let the first two bets ride, you get even money on all three bets, making your initial set of three $5 minimum bets a total of $30. If you forfeited either of your first two bets, you only get money for the bet(s) still on the table.

Of course, you can bet more than the table minimum. And if Irish eyes are smiling upon you, you can do a lot better than even money. The typical Let It Ride payout schedule is: two pair, two to one; three of a kind, three to one; straight, five to one; flush, eight to one; full house, eleven to one; four of a kind, fifty to one; straight flush, 200 to one; and royal flush, 1,000 to one. But don't get too excited. Let It Ride tables have limits that vary from casino to casino. If you're playing at a table with a $5 minimum, for example, and your cards combined with the community cards form a royal flush, you should get $15,000 if you let all your bets ride: $5 × 1,000 × 3. But you'll only get $5,000 if that's the table limit.

21: You've got a ticket to ride, and you Should care: Strategies for Let It Ride Poker

The house edge for Let It Ride is around 4 percent. It's a game in which you're going to lose some money for any bad hand, so you should make sure to play with a loss limit in mind. In this section, strategies for Let It Ride focus on the first two betting possibilities because you can take back those bets.

You can only win with a pair of tens or better. If you hold a high pair, then let your first bet ride. If you have any three cards to a royal flush—say an ace, king and jack of the same suit—then let it ride. If you have three nearly consecutive cards for a straight flush—a six, eight, and ten of the same suit—then let your first bet ride. In almost every case, if you have three consecutive cards toward a straight flush—for example, an eight, nine, and ten of the same suit—then let it ride. But if your three cards are ace, two, three or two, three, four, then consider withdrawing your first bet. Chances aren't very good that you'll be able to complete a straight flush with a low-card sequence.

When the dealer turns over his first card, you have more decisions to make. That card represents the fourth one in your hand. If the dealer's first card is a blank, one that doesn't add to the value of your hand, then you're best advised to withdraw your second bet. Let your second bet ride if you have four cards to a royal flush, straight flush, or flush. You should let it ride if the dealer's first card gives you four of a kind, three of a kind, two pair, or a pair of tens or better. And if you have four consecutive cards to a straight—with at least one high card—then let it ride.

22: PAI IN YOUR FACE: HOW TO PLAY PAI GOW POKER

Pai Gow (pronounced pie-gow) Poker is a combination of American poker and the Chinese domino game Pai Gow, a phrase that means "makes nine." In Pai Gow, you're stuck with whatever cards you're dealt. But Pai Gow differs from other poker games against the house because you're not always playing against the dealer. You play against the banker, and that position changes with every hand. Pai Gow is played at a table resembling a blackjack table, usually with room for six players. When you come up to play, you'll see at each space a number, an oval marked something like "low hand" beneath that and another oval marked "high" below that.

In Pai Gow, you're dealt seven cards, which you split into two hands, one of five cards—called the high hand—and one of two—called the low hand. A standard 52-card deck is used, and one of the jokers is left in the deck. It typically isn't used as a wild card in every situation. Its use is often limited to filling in straights, flushes, and straight flushes, or as an ace in any hand. The object of Pai Gow is to take your seven cards and create two hands that will beat the banker's two hands. Because a joker is left in the deck, the highest hand in Pai Gow Poker is five aces, which beats even a royal flush.

Once you've received your seven cards, separate them into the best possible five-two combination. But keep one thing in mind: The five-card hand MUST be stronger than the two-card hand, or you lose. It may be tempting, for example, to create a pair for your two-card hand. But if you do, and you hope to win with an ace-king high in your five-card hand, you lose. A lot of bets are "fouled" this way, so it's crucial that—no matter how many free martinis you've inhaled—you remember this fundamental rule of Pai Gow.

Once all players have created their two hands, the banker turns over her cards and creates her best two hands. A special marker called a chung is placed next to the player acting as banker because the position changes after every hand. When it's your turn to be banker, you can pass. But keeping the chung increases your odds of winning. The drawback to the position is that you have to have enough of a bankroll to cover all bets. And whether the banker is a player or the dealer, the house gets a 5 percent commission on every winning wager.

To win, you must beat both of the banker's hands. Equally ranked hands are called copies, and the banker wins all copies. If one of your hands beats the banker's and the other doesn't, the game is a push, and no money is exchanged. If you beat both of the banker's hands, then you win even money from the banker's funds—minus the house's 5 percent commission. If you've bet $25, and you beat the banker, then you win $23.75. Always bet in increments of $5. When bets aren't in those increments, the house rounds its commission to the nearest quarter, and you lose a little bit more of your winnings.

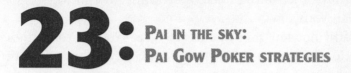

23: PAI IN THE SKY: PAI GOW POKER STRATEGIES

Forget all other poker strategy when playing Pai Gow Poker because the way to win is different from any other variety of the game. Your goal is to create not one but two hands, both of which you hope will beat the banker's. The arrangements you make have everything to do with luck being a lady tonight.

If you have seven mismatched cards and no real chance for a straight or flush, then make sure you have the highest card in your five-card hand. Put your second and third highest cards in your low hand. If you have one pair, then keep it in your five-card hand, and put your two highest single cards in your high hand. The low hand must be just that, the low hand. It cannot beat the high hand, or you lose before you even get a chance to beat the banker.

With two pair, put the higher pair in the five-card hand—unless you have an ace. Then, the smart move is to keep both pairs in the high hand and the ace in the low hand. If you have three pair, put the lowest of the three in your low hand. With two pair and a straight or flush, ignore the flush or straight and play the hand as you would two pair. If you have five cards of a straight, use them for your high hand and put the other two cards in your low hand. With six cards of a straight or flush, leave the flush or straight and put the other two cards in your low hand.

For a full house, leave the three of a kind in your high hand, and make the pair your low hand. If you have four of a kind made up of aces, kings, or queens, split the four cards into two pair, and put the lower pair in your two-card hand. If your four of a kind is jacks, tens, or nines with an ace or king, use the four of a kind as your high hand. Without an ace or a king, split the four into two pair and put the lower pair into your two-card hand. Leave any other four of a kind in your high hand. And should you be lucky enough to be dealt the nirvana of Pai Gow Poker—five aces—then it's a no-brainer. Leave three aces in your high hand and put the other two in your low hand.

Another strategy unique to Pai Gow Poker is playing the banker. Since you have to pay winning players out of your own stash, it may seem counterintuitive to be the banker—but it isn't. As banker, you win any copies. House rules on the banker's limits vary from casino to casino anyway. Some require you to cover all bets, while others will let you "play short," with less than the total of all other players' wagers. And in some places, the house limits other players' bets to what can be covered by the banker.

The best betting strategy for Pai Gow Poker is to increase your bet when you're winning and play the table minimum when losing. If you're a beginner, keep it simple. Begin by placing a bet equal to the table minimum. If you win, leave the original bet and all of your winnings. If your next hand wins, leave your original bet and add to it one chip equal to the table minimum. Keep the remainder of your winnings from the second bet. Think about it: Now you're gambling completely with the casino's money. Stick with this course until you double or halve your original bankroll.

24: WHAT THE HECK IS A BLACKJACK? THE HISTORY OF BLACKJACK

Blackjack rocks. If played correctly, the house advantage for the game is a mere .5 percent. This means that over time you'll get back $99.50 for every $100 you play. Yummy.

Like poker, the origins of blackjack are shrouded in mystery. Supposedly, it began as a French game called *vingt-et-un*, or "21." Early versions of the game sprouted up in the United States around 1800. For most of its history, people assumed blackjack was a lot like baccarat. Players couldn't do a whole lot to gain a winning advantage—that was what most folks thought, at least.

But those assumptions began to change in 1956 thanks to a team of mathematicians. An article by Baldwin, Cantey, Maisel, and McDermott in the *Journal of the American*

Statistical Association detailed a set of recommendations for play that are quite similar to the accepted wisdom of today. By following the article's advice, the house edge for blackjack could be slashed tremendously.

And then came the Bible of blackjack: *Beat the Dealer*, by MIT scientist Edward Thorp. Thorp's 1962 book introduced the concept of card counting, a process that actually gives players an advantage over the house. Thorp's brainstorm rested on two blackjack facts not previously analyzed. First, the composition of the deck changes with every hand dealt. The cards in blackjack have a "memory." Every hand dealt is dependent on what has already been dealt. Second, Thorp determined that some combinations of remaining cards favor the house, while others favor players.

He used a computer—in the days when one took up an entire building—to play tens of millions of blackjack hands and determine which circumstances produced the best odds for players. The bottom line: Tens and aces remaining in the deck are good for players, while fives and sixes are good for the house. So the way to win, Thorp argued, is to keep track of the cards. Make small bets when the remaining cards favor the dealer and large bets when they don't.

When players began to adopt Thorp's strategies en masse, casinos became understandably alarmed. For a while, rules of the game were changed to give the house back its edge. But widespread blackjack table protests and boycotts convinced casinos to bring back the game's original rules. In some cases, gambling palaces protect themselves by asking you to leave if it's clear you're counting cards. Most casinos, especially those on the Las Vegas Strip, keep their edge by using five-deck shoes at their blackjack tables. It's obviously much harder to keep track of what's left in the deck if you're dealing with 260 cards rather than fifty-two.

Many downtown Las Vegas casinos continue to offer single-deck play, as an enticement to serious gamblers. At some of the smaller downtown gambling halls, you can find blackjack tables with $1 minimums and single decks. If you're new to the game, this is an excellent way to get a cheap education in blackjack.

And as to what the heck a blackjack is? Early rules of the game awarded a player a ten to one return on his bet if his first two cards were the ace of spades ("black") and the jack of spades ("jack"). The name stuck.

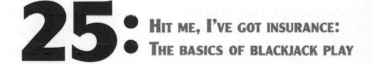

25: Hit me, I've got insurance: The basics of blackjack play

Celebrity poker tournaments may have become popular TV staples the last few years, but blackjack remains the most popular game in the casino. One reason it's popular is it's not too difficult to pick up the game's basics. But the main reason people love it is because it has great odds for players. As mentioned in number 24, the house advantage for blackjack can be as low as .5 percent. The object of blackjack is simple: Beat the dealer. You can beat her two ways: Get closer than she does to twenty-one without going over, or stay under twenty-one when the dealer busts (goes over twenty-one).

The blackjack table is a semicircle with the dealer at the center and seven players facing her. Before you sit down to play, you need to ask yourself a few questions, most of which should be answered by a sign to one side of the dealer. Does the table use a single deck of cards? Can you double down on any two cards? Can you double down after splitting pairs? Can you split pairs more than once? If the answer to all of these questions is "yes," then you've found the right table.

In blackjack, all face cards count as ten. The ace plays double duty. It can be either eleven or one, depending on what's more advantageous to you. An ace and a ten—or any face card—is an automatic winner, unless the dealer also has that hand. Then it's a push. You don't win anything, nor do you lose anything. If you're dealt twenty-one, then you're paid three to two. If your bet is $25, then you win $37.50 and your original $25 bet stays on the table. All other winners pay even money: the amount you bet plus the original bet left on the table.

The game begins when you're dealt two cards. In some casinos, the cards are dealt face-up, and in some they're face-down. When they're face-down, you hold them. If they're face-up, you don't touch them. These rules should be posted. If you hold them, then make sure you keep your other hand off the table. Otherwise, you'll be asked to remove it. After all the players have their two cards, the dealer gives herself two—one dealt face-up and one face-down.

Now it's decision time for you. Remember that the object of the game is to beat the dealer, NOT to get twenty-one. If the dealer shows a six or less, then she has to take a hit, or another card. Always assume the card the dealer has that you can't see is a ten. If she shows a six, then assume what she has is sixteen. The dealer must take a hit if she has sixteen or less. Odds are, if she takes another card she'll bust, and you win!

If the dealer shows a seven or above, then you've got to assume she has at least seventeen. If you've got a total of sixteen or less, then you'll have to take a hit until you have at least seventeen—or until you bust. If the cards are face-up, signal to the dealer you want another card by putting your fingers on the table—not on the cards—and moving them toward you. If you're holding the cards, then signal a hit by scratching the cards on the table toward you. Once you decide you've got enough cards, you're ready to stand, or let the dealer know you're satisfied with what you've got. If you're holding the cards, the signal is to place them face-down on the table under your chips. If it's a face-up game, move your hand back and forth in a wiping motion above the cards.

Blackjack also offers the option of insurance, a side bet you can make if the dealer's face-up card is an ace. And many casinos offer surrender. If you have a particularly unwelcome hand—say a total of sixteen—and the dealer shows a ten, then you may want to surrender. If you do, you lose half your bet, rather than the whole thing.

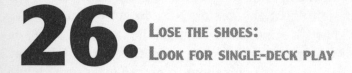

26: Lose the shoes: Look for single-deck play

One of the oldest myths of Las Vegas—it goes all the way back to the late 1940s!—is that downtown is for gamblers, and the Strip is for tourists. Strip casinos have a lock on glamour, serious gamblers say, but does a giant pyramid help you win at the tables? Strip slots are stingy, the argument continues, and rules at the tables favor players downtown. There's probably not much difference between Strip and Fremont Street slot machines. But there are grains of truth in the claim that downtown is friendlier to gamblers. It's certainly true at the blackjack tables.

Strip casinos tend to use five-deck shoes at their tables. In other words, the house uses five decks of cards instead of one. This increases the house's odds of winning because you would practically have to be a genius to be able to count cards when five decks are in play. Fewer decks also mean fewer hands played per hour, which won't help you win, but it will ensure that you don't lose as much. Also, when there are more decks, the chances of the dealer busting are reduced.

Strip casinos also tend to have higher minimums, which is fine if you want to wager a lot of money. But if you want to play for a long time without worrying about your loss limit, then downtown is the place for you.

In Las Vegas, several Fremont Street-area casinos still offer single-deck blackjack and $2-minimum tables. At some downtown casinos—the ones that might seem a little scary from the outside—you can even find $1 single-deck blackjack. If you're a total novice, then these are the places for you. You can concentrate on making the game's strategy second nature and not sweat it too much if you lose a hand here and there.

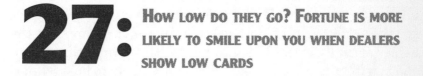

27: How low do they go? Fortune is more likely to smile upon you when dealers show low cards

One of the worst sights in a casino—other than old guys in lime-green leisure suits—is a dealer showing a nine, ten-card, or ace as her upcard at the blackjack table. If you assume—as you should—that the dealer's hole card equals ten, you should start to sweat with anything other than a natural blackjack. Think twice about splitting or doubling down. Generally speaking, your odds of winning improve when the dealer has a weak upcard showing.

If she has the seven or eight showing, she probably won't bust. But she is likely to have a very beatable seventeen or eighteen. In fact, when a dealer shows a seven, she is likely to get the weakest totals, weaker even than with stiff—or very low—upcards. If a seven is showing, then don't hesitate to split or double down with advantageous cards. If an eight is the upcard, then ask yourself just one question: "Do I feel lucky?" Well, do ya, punk? If you do, then go for it.

Who needs manna from heaven when the dealer's upcard is a four, five, or six? She will bust 42 percent of the time with these cards showing. This is the time to be aggressive, to make like a toreador with an ailing bull. Split almost anything, or double down with abandon.

If four, five, and six are great, then a two or three must be even better, right? Well, no. Wrong. Certainly you'd rather see these low cards as upcards, not an ace or a king. But the dealer actually is less likely to bust with a two or three than she is with a four, five, or six. She's only likely to bust 37 percent of the time with the two lower cards. There's still a good chance you'll win that hand if you don't bust, but play conservatively. Get a total of at least seventeen and stand pat.

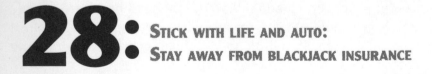

28: Stick with life and auto: Stay away from blackjack insurance

Insurance is a good thing when a tree falls on your house or when a little old lady who can't see above the steering wheel plays bumper cars with your SUV. It's not a good thing at the blackjack table. It's not quite a sucker bet, but it's close.

Insurance is a side bet. To make it, you have to place an additional wager on the insurance line that's worth half your initial bet. If your bet is, say $10, then you've got to place a $5 chip on the insurance space. There are two reasons why you could go for insurance. The first is because the dealer's show card is an ace. Your assumption needs to be that he's got a ten or face card hidden and, therefore, a natural winner. If it turns out that he does, then you come out ahead because your insurance bet pays two to one.

The other reason you might be tempted to make this side bet is related to the first. The dealer shows an ace, and you have a natural. If it turns out he does have twenty-one—and you do too—then the result is a push. You don't lose, but you don't win anything either. But if both you and the dealer have twenty-one and you've taken out insurance, then you lose your initial bet, but your insurance bet pays two to one. So when you bet $10 and then $5 for insurance, you come out ahead $5.

But insurance is a bad bet because most of the time the dealer does not have blackjack when he's showing an ace. Think of it this way: If you take away your ten-ace combo and the ace the dealer holds, then of the forty-nine cards left, fifteen will give the dealer a natural. But thirty-four of them will give the dealer a lesser hand. Remember that insurance pays two to one, but blackjack pays three to two. Therefore, not insuring your natural means you'll win 150 percent of your bet thirty-four times and push fifteen times. After several hands of play, this averages out to you winning 104 percent of your bet on average by not insuring.

The only exception to the "no insurance" rule is if you're a card counter. If you're counting cards and know with certainty the dealer has a ten or face card in the hole—and you don't have a natural—then go for insurance and win your two to one bet.

29: Seeing seeing or not seeing double: The art of doubling down

One of the funniest moments in the great 1996 film *Swingers* is when the hapless Mike bets his entire bankroll on a high-stakes blackjack table. No surprise, since the film is about two best friends who spend their time looking for "beautiful babies" in Las Vegas and L.A. Mike wants to impress . . . anyone. He sits down at a blackjack table without paying attention to the minimum bet and—rather than admit his mistake—he stays at the table and then doubles down, wagering everything he's brought with him. He loses, of course. After that, his buddy Trent good-naturedly mocks him with the nickname "Double Down."

Mike may lose the hand, but his thinking is on target. Doubling down is generally a good thing for a player to do.

Doubling down is a bet added onto your original wager. You double your original wager by sliding a second to the side of the original bet, to tell the dealer you want to double down. She'll give you one card and no more. Let's say, for example, that you're dealt a six and a five, and the dealer's show card is a six. You indicate to the dealer that you want to double down, and you're dealt a ten or face card. Score! You've got twenty-one. It's not a natural, but so what? Provided the dealer busts or gets less than twenty-one herself, you win. If you bet $5, then doubled down with another $5, your total return is $10 plus the original bets. Virtually all casinos allow you to double down if you have a total of eleven or ten. At some, you can double down with nine or more. Some casinos even allow you to double down on any two cards.

In casinos that allow doubling down with any cards you're holding, the general rules are as follows. Double down if:

- You have eleven and the dealer shows two through ten.
- You have ten and the dealer shows two through nine.
- You have nine and the dealer shows three through six. This is called doubling with "hard hands" because you don't have an ace. (An ace counts as one or eleven in blackjack.)

You should also consider doubling down on so-called "soft hands," those that include an ace. In that case, double down if:

- You have an ace and a six or seven and the dealer shows three through six.
- You have an ace and a five or four and the dealer's show card is four through six.
- You have an ace and a three or two, and the dealer shows a five or six.

If a casino allows you to double down after splitting pairs then remember to split your pairs first. (For more on splitting pairs, read on to the next point.)

30: Splitting hairs, er, pairs: The art of splitting pairs

Splitting pairs is an additional blackjack bet that's generally advantageous to the player. If you're dealt two cards of the same value, you can signal to the dealer that you want to split the pairs by laying down an additional bet equal to your original bet. When you split pairs, you get to play these original cards as two separate hands. Unlike doubling down, you can take as many cards as you believe are necessary to create two good hands.

The best opportunity for splitting comes when you have two aces. Instead of one hand totaling a sucky twelve, you've got the chance to get two hands both worth twenty-one. In most casinos, if you're dealt a third card of the same value, then you can lay down one more bet and split a third time. Most casinos also offer the chance to double down on split hands, when appropriate. For example, let's say you're dealt two eights, giving you a terrible total of sixteen. If you split your pair, you now have the chance to get two pairs worth eighteen. This hand is much more likely to make you a winner. After you've split, let's say your first card is an ace, giving you a total of nineteen for that hand. Stand pat. Then, on your second eight, let's say you're dealt a three. Make an additional wager, equal to your original bet, to let the dealer know you want to double down on that hand. Now you've got a pretty good chance to make blackjack.

When do you split pairs? The answer is: Split pairs when it's advantageous to you. It's not advantageous to split tens or face cards because that pair gives you a total of twenty, a difficult hand for the dealer to beat, whatever upcard he shows. If you split the tens and wind up with two pairs of twenty, then you're golden. But the odds don't favor you, and remember that old adage about a bird in the hand.

The principles for splitting pairs are as follows:

- Always split aces, always.
- Never split tens or face cards.
- Split two nines, if the dealer's upcard is two through nine—unless the dealer shows a seven. Why? For the same reason you shouldn't split tens. If you have two

nines, then you've got a total of eighteen. If the dealer shows a seven, then you have to assume he's holding a ten. Your odds are better of beating the probable seventeen with your two cards totaling eighteen.

- Split two eights, no matter what, because a total of sixteen is among the worst hands you can have in blackjack.
- Split when you have two sevens and the dealer shows a two through seven.
- Split if you have two sixes and the dealer shows two through six.
- Never split fives. Play them straight or double down.
- Split if you have two fours and the dealer shows a five or six.
- Split if you have two threes or two twos and the dealer shows two through seven.

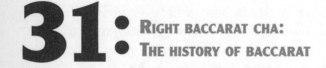

31: Right baccarat cha: The history of baccarat

Baccarat is another of those games for which numerous possible histories exist. The word is both French and Italian for "zero," which is what you end up with when you wager money on it. Just kidding. In baccarat, face cards and tens count as zero. Since the word has origins in both countries, both nations try to claim baccarat as their creation.

One commonly held story of baccarat's origin is that it was invented in Italy in the Middle Ages and played with a deck of Tarot cards. Others claim the game traces its origins to the French game vingt-et-un ("21"), the same game from which blackjack developed. Since baccarat does bear some resemblance to blackjack, it's tempting to ascribe the game a French origin. Some histories claim the game was invented in Italy as a scrambled form of vingt-et-un.

Whether its origins are Italian or French—or both—baccarat was wildly popular in European casinos before it was imported to Las Vegas, by way of pre-Castro Cuban casinos. It got—and to some extent keeps—the reputation for being an elegant game for high rollers only—it's the game James Bond plays when he goes to a casino.

Baccarat first showed up in Las Vegas in the 1950s, at the long-gone Dunes Casino. The aura of sophistication remained, and to this day, you'll likely see well-dressed, well-off gentlemen and ladies gathered in groups around the baccarat tables. In recent years, some casinos have begun taking steps to deglamorize baccarat, or at least to make it less off-putting to casual gamblers.

Baccarat really is one of the simpler games in the casino because it uses a specific set of rules that leave players little to do except sit back and watch. Blackjack requires a great deal of strategy, and it's very popular. Casinos figure if people realize they don't have to break open their piggy banks and take out third mortgages to play baccarat, then they'll line up once they understand the game's simplicity. One way casinos are working to attract players to the game is by introducing mini-baccarat. The "mini" refers to the table, which is smaller and less daunting. This version also has lower-limit stakes. The average minimum for mini-baccarat is $5, the same as the minimum for blackjack at most Strip casinos.

Baccarat and mini-baccarat are games of chance, not of skill, but they have house odds that are pretty good to players: between 1.17 percent and 1.36 percent. So if you want to play-act that you're Bond, James Bond, then baccarat may be a good game to try. Walk up, order a vodka martini—shaken not stirred, of course—and play.

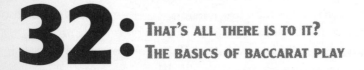

32: That's all there is to it? The basics of baccarat play

The objective of baccarat is to bet on the winning hand. The winning hand is the one closest to a total of nine. OK, it's a little more complicated than that, but not much. In baccarat, face cards and tens count as zero, and aces count as one. No matter how many players are at the table, only two hands are dealt, both face-up on the table: one for the dealer, or banker, and one that represents the player. In front of each player at the baccarat table are three rectangles, one for bets on the banker, one for bets on the player, and one for ties.

Cards are dealt out of a shoe, usually containing six to eight decks. To begin play, place your bet on one of the rectangles. Then sit back and see if you've won. Take a drink. Think about baseball. Just chill—unless you become the dealer. In baccarat, the shoe is passed around from player to player. A player holds the shoe until the player hand beats the dealer hand.

The winning hand is the one closest to nine. Even though face cards count as zero, it's still possible for two cards to go over nine. If they do, then subtract ten for the true number. If one of the hands totals nine—a four and five, a six and three, a seven and two, an ace and an eight—it's called a natural. If you bet on that hand, you win. A hand that totals eight also is called a natural—or if you're a fancy pants—*le petit* natural. If you're using French, then a nine is *le grand* natural.

After the two cards are dealt for the player and for the banker, the "call man"—a casino employee—will tell the player with the shoe who gets the next card, if one is merited. There are strict rules for when a hand gets an additional card, and it's never more than one card per hand. If a hand is a natural, then that's it. If neither hand is a natural, then the simple rules of baccarat get a bit more complicated. But you don't have to do anything. The call man guides you through the process.

The call man always starts with the player hand. If it totals zero through five, then another card is dealt. If it's higher than five, the player stands. The outcome of the player hand determines how the banker plays his hand. If the player has a natural, the banker does not draw a card regardless of the hand's total. If the player stands with a six or seven, the banker hand must draw a card if the two-card total is zero through five. The banker hand stands if the total is six or more.

When the player hand draws a third card, the banker hand draws a card if:

- The total is two or less.
- The total is three and the player hand has an ace, two, three, four, five, six, seven, nine, or ten.
- The total is four and the player hand has a two, three, four, five, six, or seven.
- The total is five and the player hand has a four, five, six, or seven.
- The total is six and the player hand has a six or seven.

The banker hand always stands if the hand is seven.

After all of this, the hand closest to nine wins. If the two hands end in a tie, then those who bet on a tie win even money. Players who bet on the player or banker hand don't lose or win any money. If the player hand wins and you bet on the player, you get even money. A winning bet on the banker wins even money, minus 5 percent, which goes to the house.

33: Don't chart a giant course: Avoid filling out charts and looking like a simp

Casinos are masters at making games of chance seem like games of skill, thus giving you the illusion that you can control luck. In the bingo parlor, for example, players are welcome to keep amulets and good luck charms. Why not? Your stinky "lucky" socks won't really affect how the numbers come up. But if you believe they will, then you'll play. Baccarat tables also have a gimmick: the scorecard.

Casinos are only too happy to give players blank scorecards and pens that have black ink on one end and red on the other. The cards are marked with alternating "p's" (for player) and "b's" (for banker). The standard method for filling out these charts is to use one color for "p" and one for "b." The purpose of these cards, ostensibly, is to detect patterns of play. If the player wins three times in a row, then you might want to wager on the player again. Of course, some players would say the banker's now due for a win, so bet on him. If you talk to folks who fill out these charts, you might be convinced by there's something to charting. Charting aficionados swear they've used charts to predict the outcome of many a baccarat hand with eerie accuracy. They have the zeal of born-again Christians.

But this is a game of chance we're talking about, not the fate of your immortal soul. And a game of chance is ruled by chance alone. Baccarat charts only tell you who has won previous hands. They don't predict future hands with any certainty. Just because the banker wins three times in a row and then the player wins three times in a row, it doesn't mean the banker will win the next game. What happens in one hand has no bearing on the next hand. But if filling out a scorecard makes you feel secure, then do it. Just remember to stick to your loss limit when the expected patterns don't appear.

34: Making something out of nothing: Betting strategies for baccarat

Most gambling books gloss over sections about baccarat strategy, noting simply that baccarat is a game of chance with fixed rules and, therefore, little opportunity for strategy. But if you're one of those folks who believe strategy of some sort is a must before you play any game, then baccarat expert and author Brian Kayser may be your saving grace. He offers a basic strategy and some advanced strategies he claims have proven effective.

Kayser's basic strategy says bet one chip that two wins in a row by the banker or the player will not make three in a row. If you lose three times in a row, bet three chips that two in a row will not make three in a row. If you lose that bet, repeat the whole sequence. If you again lose four bets, wait for the next shoe—this one obviously carries some bad mojo. The advantage of the system, Kayser says, is that it keeps you from having to bet every hand, increasing the amount of your bet when odds are in your favor. Also, this strategy slows down play, making it less likely you'll make a mistake.

Some gamblers don't like the idea of cashing in whatever chips they have left after four losing bets, so Kayser offers them an advanced strategy. If you're using his basic strategy and you lose two series of four bets, then bet twelve chips that two player or banker wins will not make three. Quit if you win. If you lose, however, bet twenty-four units that two will not make three. Continue in the same manner, and double your bet until you break even. Then quit. The drawback to this system is that if it's not effective, you'll lose a bundle.

Another of Kayser's advanced strategies involves betting against a trend. If either the player or banker has won eight hands in a row, then bet against the run. Each time you lose, bet against the run again, doubling your last bet and adding one more chip. Do not bet against runs if they start from the middle of the shoe. Once again, the drawback to this system is that it could cost you a pretty penny. Kayser warns that you need to be financially prepared to lose *at least* eight bets in a row.

Kayser's final advanced strategy is basically the opposite of his second. After the player or banker wins four hands in a row, bet a chip that the run will make five. Let that bet ride to nine in a row. If you make nine, then take your money off the table and put back whatever amount you choose. Go for ten in a row. As the run continues, keep following step two until you lose. Don't use the strategy if the shoe is low, and if it makes you more comfortable, you can let your bet ride to just six in a row before removing your winnings.

35: Why baccarat is boring if played correctly: Always bet on the banker

For all its air of sophistication and glamour, baccarat is really a pretty simple game, about as challenging as that old childhood staple, Chutes and Ladders. Some professionals suggest a variety of betting strategies, but these are designed for serious players. If you're a casual gambler, then you don't need to concern yourself with abstruse strategy or attempts at card counting: Just bet on the banker.

The winning hand in baccarat pays even money. In 100 hands of baccarat, the probability of a player's hand winning is around 49.3 percent, while the banker's hand will win 50.7 percent. Casinos try to level those odds by charging a 5 percent commission on each banker's bet. You don't pay the commission after every round—the dealer keeps track of it and collects at the end of a shoe or when the player leaves the table. If you win $100, for example, then you need to give the dealer $5 if you bet solely on the banker. You don't have to pay a commission when you bet on the player's hand.

Well, you might say, that's a raw deal. Why the heck would I bet on the banker when I have to give up some of my not-so-hard-earned money? After all, the difference in odds is only a little more than 1 percent. Well, here's why you should do it. Even with the 5 percent commission, you're likely to lose less money betting on the banker than betting on the player. If it's a standard 5 percent commission it breaks down like this: When you bet $100 over the course of 100 hands, you are likely to lose $1.30 by betting on the player. But you would only lose $1.17, even after the commission, if you bet on the banker each time.

Banker and player aren't the only wagers in baccarat, but the other is a sucker bet: the tie. Odds are that a tie in baccarat will occur only once every ten hands, if that. The bet pays eight to one, a good payout. But the house advantage for the tie bet is 14 percent or more, and that edge is beyond rotten compared with the 1.17 percent for banker bets and the 1.36 percent for player bets. Unless you're feeling extremely lucky—or extremely crazy—stay away from the tie bet.

LOUNGE ACT

Viva Las Vegas . . .
What You Didn't Know about
the History of Sin City

Your first lounge act will take you on a rapid journey through the history of Las Vegas, which celebrated its centennial in 2005. In its earliest years, the town was often in danger of not making it in the middle of the twentieth century, much less into the dawn of the twenty-first with a population approaching 2,000,000 people. Its founders wouldn't recognize the place.

Or would they? From its earliest years, the Las Vegas's remoteness gave it a unique character. It was a city where mavericks could make fortunes by taking big chances, and that's still true today. Just replace Montana Senator William Clark—after whom Las Vegas's Clark County was named—with Bugsy Siegel or Howard Hughes or Jay Sarno or Steve

Wynn. Once Nevada legalized gambling in 1931, Las Vegas began to attract visitors from near and far. While the Hoover Dam was being built, workers left their company town of Boulder City to live it up in Sin City.

One thing can be said about the town known variously as Sin City, the Entertainment Capital of the World, and simply Vegas(!): It's a survivor constantly reinventing itself. It's a thoroughly modern city with a personality so unique it continues to enchant people from all over the world. It's a city that has darkness in its past—Mafia connections, racism—yet it's known to most as a city of lights and magic.

So mix up a martini—lounge acts almost always have a two-drink minimum, you know—and wait for the curtain to rise. First you'll travel from Las Vegas's Native American origins to the city's birth in 1905. Then you'll watch as a dying city is resurrected by a massive federal government project that remains to this day one of the world's great engineering marvels. After that, you'll meet Benjamin "Bugsy" Siegel, who transformed an ugly duckling of sawdust joints into a golden swan of gambling palaces—and helped to make a small highway a few miles from town become one of the world's most famous streets.

Then you'll spend some time with the Bashful Billionaire, Howard Hughes, who single-handedly removed the mob from Sin City and replaced it with a new mob of corporate middlemen seeking higher and higher bottom lines. Finally, you'll take a look at Las Vegas's recent history: Yes, it transformed yet again—this time, into a family-friendly destination. But the city is already in the process of changing back to a place just for adults. Viva Las Vegas, indeed.

36: HANGING OUT AT BLOCK 16: LAS VEGAS IS BORN

No, "Las Vegas" doesn't mean, as some comedians have said, "Lost Wages." It means "the meadows." Its name comes from the meadows formed by the freshwater springs that made the desert oasis an ideal stop for trains. Even before there were iron horses, the region got its name from Spanish traders who found the springs after they strayed from the Old Spanish Trail.

And long before there were Spanish traders or $3 buffets marked the Las Vegas valley, it was home to the Anasazi, a Native American tribe that disappeared from the area around 1150 A.D. Centuries later—in the mid-1800s—Mormons made the first attempt to create a permanent settlement out of Las Vegas.

Then, in 1905, Montana Senator William Clark created a town to serve as a way station for his San Pedro, Los Angeles & Salt Lake Railroad. A public auction was held on May 15 and 16 at a train station, now the site of Jackie Gaughan's Plaza Hotel and Casino. Clark sold 1,800 acres of lots for bids as high as $1,750. Not bad money in those days, but nothing compared to cost of Las Vegas real estate today.

Block 16 was early Las Vegas's most popular block. That's because when the 1,800 acres were sold, there was one stipulation: None of the blocks, except 16, could have saloons. Yep, in its earliest days as a town, the future Sin City was under self-imposed prohibition. Block 16 was not only the place to put mud in your eye, it also was the spot where traveling businessmen, far from home, could purchase temporary, intimate companionship.

Many early settlers gave up on the town. It was subject to flash floods, desert heat, and harsh winds. If a fire broke out, it spread like, well, wildfire. By 1911, Las Vegas had about 1,500 permanent residents, most of whom made their living from two railroads that crisscrossed the town—both owned by Clark. One of those lines, the Las Vegas & Tonopah, was built to serve mines discovered north of Las Vegas. When the precious metals began to dry up, the Las Vegas & Tonopah did too. It went broke in 1917, leaving many jobless.

And then Las Vegas's founding father, William Clark, abandoned his dusty ship. He sold the San Pedro, Los Angeles & Salt Lake to the Union Pacific Railroad. By the close of the 1920s, Las Vegas seemed likely to follow other boom-and-bust communities like Rhyolite or Goldfield, which became twentieth century ghost towns.

But Sin City, which seems to have more lives than the hardiest house cat, was saved for the first time by one of the nation's biggest projects—a dam site.

37:
A dam raises a little hell:
The construction of Boulder Dam

Without the Colorado River, there probably wouldn't be any Las Vegas, or any metropolises in Southern California. The river is the lifeline of the desert, supplying energy and water to millions. But the river could also be unpredictable and challenging to hardy West Coast residents of the nineteenth and early twentieth centuries.

The year Las Vegas was founded, the Colorado flooded and destroyed millions of dollars of crops in California's Imperial Valley. A few years later, it practically dried up, dwindling to a dusty trickle and again endangering farmers' livelihoods.

The United States Department of the Interior's Reclamation Service Branch decided to build a dam to control the Colorado River's power. Two sites twenty miles apart seemed most promising for the project: Boulder Canyon and Black Canyon. Reconnaissance teams decided Black Canyon was more stable, and it's a good thing too. Black Canyon is a mere thirty miles from the train station where Las Vegas began, and the constant stream of scientists and politicians who began pulling into the station must have made tongues wag over bootleg liquor at every saloon along Block 16.

In 1928, Las Vegas residents learned what was going on. President Calvin Coolidge signed the Boulder Canyon Project Act in 1928, which set the construction of the Boulder Dam in motion. It's unclear why the project and the dam were named after the site that was NOT chosen for its construction. When out-of-work residents heard the news, the question became Federal Prohibition? What Prohibition? Bootleg liquor flowed, and revelers partied for days.

Las Vegans assumed their town would become home to the tens of thousands of workers who constructed the dam once the project began in 1931. In an effort to come across like a fine, upstanding town, Las Vegas leaders forced illegal saloons to close their doors and asked prostitutes to stay—alone—behind closed doors whenever government officials came to visit. The ruse didn't work. It's just not in Las Vegas's blood to be respectable. The federal government opted to create a model town, Boulder City, close to the dam site.

But Las Vegas remained a lure for dam workers, especially after March 19, 1931, when Nevada became the first state to legalize gambling, and the "illegal" gaming houses in Las Vegas could finally run out in the open. In due time, other sawdust joints with legal games of chance popped up, and dam workers frequently left their homes in Boulder City for what passed in those days for the bright lights of Vegas. They had to if they wanted to try their luck. To this day, Boulder City is the only spot in Nevada without gambling.

On September 30, 1935, President Franklin D. Roosevelt dedicated "Boulder Dam," even though Congress had named it Hoover Dam—after President Herbert Hoover—before construction began. But most folks continued to call the nearly $50 million project Boulder Dam, despite the fact that it wasn't actually built in Boulder Canyon. Congress restored the official name in 1947, and Hoover Dam became—and has remained—a favorite tourist attraction for travelers.

The dam regulates the flow of the Colorado River. But when first constructed, it also served another purpose, one the Bureau of Reclamation hadn't foreseen. The Hoover Dam saved Las Vegas after many workers decided to remain in the town once work on the dam was complete.

38: You want to put it where? Las Vegas becomes high class

To many visitors, the Strip IS Las Vegas. Serious gamblers tend to flock downtown, believing that the odds in Fremont Street casinos are superior to those along Las Vegas Boulevard. But vacationers with a casual gambling jones will probably find themselves along the roughly three-mile stretch of heavily congested road that begins at Tropicana Avenue and ends at Sahara Avenue.

Just a little more than sixty years ago, however, visitors could have stood on the site of Caesars Palace and seen nothing but tumbling tumbleweeds and the occasional car zipping by on what was then called the Los Angeles Highway. Fremont Street—the heart of Las Vegas—was three miles away. Unless you enjoyed rattlesnakes and shoes full of sand, you'd have been crazy to do anything other than drive quickly past all that vacant desert on the way to Fremont.

Then Los Angeles hotelier Tom Hull got an idea. He saw those cars driving down the Los Angeles Highway and thought, "Why not give them a reason to stop?" He bought up 33 acres at the—then—very generous sum of $150 an acre and got ready to build. Hull already had a series of hotels in the Southwest that bore the name "El Rancho." In 1941, he added the El Rancho Vegas to his empire. Townspeople applauded Hull's daring. It's likely they also thought he was nuts.

But Las Vegas visitors were attracted by the large neon windmill atop the El Rancho, and by its swimming pools and horseback-riding trails. Soon, Las Vegans knew Hull *was* crazy . . . like a fox. The El Rancho expanded to 220 rooms. Movie theater mogul R. E. Griffith followed Hull's lead in 1942 and opened the Last Frontier. It had a Wild West theme and boasted a bar taken from one of Block 16's original saloons.

The El Rancho and the Last Frontier were successful, but they certainly were not glamorous. They were nicely accommodated, family-friendly motels. In both, the casinos were small, almost an afterthought.

A petty criminal turned hitman for the Mob changed the way Las Vegas is run, and his influence can be felt to this day. Benjamin "Bugsy" Siegel was often sent to Los Angeles "on business." Sometimes, he'd take a side trip to Las Vegas, and he enjoyed gambling in the El Rancho and the Last Frontier. But these guys were doing it all wrong, Bugsy thought. In 1945, he began to plan a more elaborate, glitzy property at which the casino would be the star.

Bugsy gained the financial backing of his "business partners," Lucky Luciano and Meyer Lansky, who bankrolled the Flamingo for $1 million. Bugsy took over a casino project that went bust out on the Los Angeles Highway and had a vision for a gambling palace that would be in the same league as elaborate Miami resorts. The extravagance Bugsy put into the Flamingo cost him his life. He quickly went through the first million, then another, then another. All totaled, the project racked up to around $6 million.

The nail in Bugsy's coffin was opening day, December 26, 1946. It was a wet, wintry day, and most of the Hollywood stars who said they'd come out to meet and greet Flamingo guests decided to stay in sunnier Los Angeles. In addition, the casino was first-class, but the motel wasn't even finished. Guests had to stay at other Las Vegas properties. The Flamingo closed after two weeks. He reopened it later, and things began to look better. But soon after its reopening, Bugsy was shot to death in Los Angeles, as he sat in his girlfriend Virginia Hill's home reading the *Los Angeles Times*.

It was the end of Bugsy Siegel, but it wasn't the end of the Flamingo. Another gangland figure, Gus Greenbaum, arrived in the casino just minutes after Bugsy was left dead in a pool of blood. Greenbaum had extensive experience with—illegal—gambling management, and his experience quickly made Bugsy's dream come true of a posh gambling Mecca with world-class entertainment and high rollers galore. It was the beginning of Las Vegas's reputation as the seventh heaven of sophisticated gambling destinations. Bugsy's vision turned out to be iron solid, but he was too busy sleeping with the fishes to enjoy his validation.

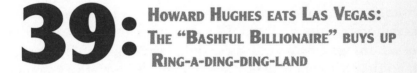

39: Howard Hughes eats Las Vegas: The "Bashful Billionaire" buys up Ring-a-ding-ding-land

What do you do when you have $546,549,171 burning a hole in your pocket? If you're Howard Hughes, you decide to transform Las Vegas from La Cosa Nostra West into a legitimate vacationland.

Hughes famously entered Las Vegas in the dead of night on November 27, 1966. An express train he had boarded in Boston ran into mechanical difficulties in Utah, so Hughes paid for a locomotive to take his private cars the rest of the way to Sin City. Hughes was taken off the train, loaded onto a stretcher and put into a waiting van for a short ride to the Desert Inn. He didn't leave his room there for four years.

Hughes was the "Bashful Billionaire" of legend by the time he was taken off the train. The once-dashing aviator and movie mogul who squired some of Tinsel Town's hottest leading ladies had become a gaunt, addicted shadow. A serious plane crash left him in constant pain, and he relieved that pain with narcotics.

Hughes may not have been much to look at, but he had everything he needed to build an empire: lots and lots of money. In May of 1966, Hughes sold his controlling interest in Trans World Airlines for nearly $550 million. He wanted to take that money and go to a place where it wouldn't be taxed down to nothing, and Las Vegas seemed like just the place. He already owned some land far from the city limits, land that today is home to the exclusive Summerlin community. And one of the pictures he produced was *The Las Vegas Story*, which was filmed partly in Bugsy Siegel's Flamingo.

Hughes moved into the Desert Inn and took over its top two floors. His aides told the casino's owners—including Mob associate Moe Dalitz—that Hughes would move on after Christmas. But he didn't. When hotel managers asked Hughes to leave, he bought the hotel/casino for $13.2 million instead. The Hughes era of Las Vegas had begun.

The billionaire wanted to make Las Vegas a legitimate town, free of the taint of Mob affiliation.

But that's not to say he wanted Las Vegas to become home to Hiltons, MGM's and Holiday Inns. Hughes may have founded Trans World Airlines, a huge corporation, but he was certainly no man in the gray flannel suit. In effect, Hughes was the god-father of casino entrepreneurs like Bob Stupak, Jay Sarno, and Steve Wynn. As Hughes's lifestyle suggested, he liked the idea of having total control over properties he owned.

In rapid succession, those properties included the Sands, the Castaways, the Frontier, the Silver Slipper, and the Land-mark. Legend has it that he bought the tiny Silver Slipper for one reason only: to get rid of that damned slipper. The casino was directly across from the Desert Inn, and its trademark was a giant, garishly lit, revolving slipper atop the property's sign. The slipper kept Hughes awake. A quick $5,360,000 took care of that problem. The slipper resides today in the so-called Neon Graveyard outside of Las Vegas's YESCO sign company. Hughes also bought a small airline and a local television station.

Hughes's casino properties lost money, most likely because of crooked practices within them, some of which were perpe-trated by Hughes associates. He couldn't have the complete control he craved, and besides, there was talk of a hydrogen bomb test in the desert hundreds of miles from Las Vegas. A news story said that folks on upper floors of casino proper-ties might feel a slight earth tremor.

So, in the wee hours of November 1970, Hughes left Las Vegas. He was again carried on a stretcher, but this time he left from nearby Nellis Air Force Base aboard his private jet, bound for the Bahamas. The Hughes era was over.

40: PARENTS IN WONDERLAND: SIN CITY GOES FAMILY-FRIENDLY

If Bugsy Siegel brought the sheen of glamour to Las Vegas, then Jay Sarno brought the sprinkling of magic. He also built the first family-friendly casino on the Strip,

Caesars Palace, in 1966. There was no apostrophe here; for Sarno, this implied that every visitor was a Caesar. It was like nothing the city had seen. Yes, it was elegant and glitzy. But it was no mere Fabulous Flamingo. In some ways, Caesars was a return to the Strip's roots. The Last Frontier had a Wild West theme—appropriate for a western town whose early heart was a block filled with saloons and prostitutes.

But Caesars was something else altogether—ancient Rome transplanted to the middle of the desert. The property boasted Roman columns, sculpture, statues, a giant Caesar pointing out to the Strip as though hailing a cab, and—in its earliest days—cocktail waitresses in togas who greeted customers with the words, "Welcome to Caesars Palace. I am your slave."

In 1969, Sarno opened another elaborate casino. While Caesars spoke to the desire for power in us all, Circus Circus spoke to the child in all of us. Built in the shape of a giant pink big top, Circus Circus offered gambling, of course. But it also offered carnival games for the kids and trapeze artists flying over the heads of folks waiting to double down.

Sarno was so sure Circus Circus would be a magnet for Las Vegas visitors that he opened it without a hotel and charged an entrance fee to anyone who lived outside of the city. Gamblers stayed away in droves. Sarno sold Circus Circus in 1974 to William G. Bennett, who made some minor changes—like getting rid of the entrance fee—and the property became a huge draw. It was the one casino in Sin City where parents could gamble their mortgages away while their kids entertained themselves with games and circus acts on the casino's second floor.

Sarno's vision took hold. The Las Vegas of today is awash with colorful fantasy palaces in the shape of pyramids—the Luxor; fairy castles—Circus Circus Enterprises's Excalibur; the New York City skyline—New York, New York, a joint venture of MGM and Circus Circus; and Venetian landmarks, The Venetian.

Other entrepreneurs with an eye for the grand scale of today's Las Vegas soon followed Sarno's lead. Kirk Kerkorian built the International and the original MGM Grand. Steve Wynn combined the majesty of Kerkorian's properties with the fantasy aspect of Sarno's.

In 1988, Wynn built the Mirage, which outglitzed even its neighbor, Caesars Palace. He added a volcano outside, which erupted every few minutes in a tumble of flame and soaring music. Next to the Mirage, Wynn built Treasure Island, with a pirate theme that appealed to all ages. For years, the property boasted the best free show on the Strip. Every hour, the lagoon in front of Treasure Island was the site of a battle between the British and a band of rascally pirates. The pirates won of course, sending the British ship to the bottom of the fake lagoon. Finally, Wynn brought the Bellagio to the Strip. Its massive fountains dance to the accompaniment of opera, matching the brilliance of the Mirage's flames.

By the mid-1990s, Las Vegas was filled with resorts that offered something for both adults and children. Marketing campaigns implied that Sin City wasn't really so sinful—it was Disneyland for all ages. But that image is shifting again, as Las Vegas plays up its role as America's id, the one spot in the nation where anything goes.

PART 3:

ROLLING BONES AND BETTING ON BLACK:
CRAPS AND ROULETTE

CRAPS TAKES THE PRIZE FOR LOUDEST GAME IN THE CASINO. Poker is full of, well, poker-faced players busy concentrating and plotting strategy. And since the money you win at poker is taken from other players, you're best off not shouting and gloating while you're raking in your opponents' chips. Baccarat is full of grim-faced high rollers. Blackjack also takes concentration and focus, so it's not a chatty game.

But craps? Oh yeah, baby. With every toss of the dice, some folks win and some lose. Every toss is a drama or comedy at triple speed. People shout or groan. It's the best of times and the worst of times. And you don't even have to be the shooter to be part of the show. Heck, you don't even have to be a bettor to appreciate the game, but watching it is particularly exciting when you've got hard-earned cash riding on two little pieces of see-through plastic.

The game can be off-putting to beginners because of its sheer number of bets bearing bizarre names. So, after a little history, you'll find out the basics of play. The game is really quite simple, as are the bets, once they're defined. You'll learn which bets are good ones and which should be avoided. You'll discover the importance of streaking, and get a fix on some of the superstitions that surround craps. No game of chance, except for bingo, has so many.

After spending time in the land of craps, you'll move on to the world of roulette. Serious gamblers often avoid the game, leaving it for newcomers who aren't aware of how high the house advantage is for just about every bet. But you'll learn that roulette can be an enjoyable, leisurely game, with an air of sophistication similar to baccarat, only less snooty. You'll discover strategies to help you win—or at least not lose as much—and then learn why American roulette can be a great excuse for traveling to Europe.

41: COME, DON'T COME. SEE IF I CARE: THE HISTORY OF CRAPS

Craps is the fastest-paced game in a casino, and it generates excitement like the Hoover Dam generates electricity. No other game elicits as many cries of lusty joy and groans of lugubrious dejection. And few games have had such an impact on our lexicon and culture: roll them bones, snake eyes, lucky seven, the green felt jungle, aw crap. Okay, maybe not that last one.

Dice games have been around since the dawn of humankind. They've been used to determine a course of action set by the gods, along the lines of, "Whose still-beating heart would you like to see next, oh mighty one?" And sometimes dice have been used for the same reason they are used today—to give people a chance to drink, smoke, and gamble away their children's inheritance. Ancient Romans and Native American tribes played games with cubes they fashioned out of animal bones, hence the expression "roll them bones." Dice have also been made out of ivory and porcelain, but these opaque materials invite cheaters to load dice. Them bones are made out of translucent cellulose today.

Gambling historians believe craps began as an Arab game, which reached Europe under the name "hazard." The French brought it to the New World in the eighteenth century.

The game's colorful name is a variation of "crebs" or "crabes," the lowest-value roll in hazard. It became a popular game on gambling riverboats in the nineteenth century. In those days, the game had only field and come bets (more about them later). Dice-maker John H. Winn (great name for gambling, John!) introduced new variations that allowed players to make bets with or against the dice. By the early part of the twentieth century, Winn's innovations were so popular that they led to craps as we know it today. But the game's modern popularity can also be traced to World War II, when soldiers played the game to pass time.

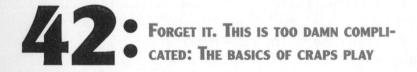

42: Forget it. This is too damn complicated: The basics of craps play

The lightning-quick pace of craps can be daunting to first-time players, but the game's rules are pretty simple. It's the table terms and bets that make the game seem complicated and intimidating.

Craps is played at a large table and requires four casino personnel. Only one player is needed, but the tables can usually accommodate fifteen or more players. At the center of the table—on opposite sides of the table—are the stickman and boxman. The stickman is the showman of the game. He handles the dice with a rattan stick. He offers new players a number of dice, from which you choose the two that feel lucky. After each roll of the dice, the stickman announces the number thrown and probably describes its consequences. The stickman also keeps up with bets. If he's good, he'll also keep up a good run of patter to make the proceedings light and exciting. The boxman is the craps cop. She sits at the center of the table between the game's two dealers. She supervises the running of the table, watching the casino's bankroll like a hawk and settling disputes between dealers and players.

Craps uses two dealers, who stand on either side of the boxman at opposite ends of the table. In front of the dealers are various rectangles, squares, and circles that demarcate the variety of available bets. The designs are identical at both ends of the table. The dealers handle all bets at their ends of the table, paying off winning ones, taking away losing ones. Both dealers also have what's called a "marker buck," a plastic disk indicating the established point—or number thrown by the player. The dealer is the ambassador of craps. She's the one to whom players address most questions, and she is a player's main point of contact throughout a game.

But wait, there are more . . . casino personnel, that is. Craps tables are assembled around a central area known as the pit. Floormen spend entire shifts on their feet supervising individual tables or groups of tables. The big daddy, the god of craps, is the pit boss. The floormen work under him, and he's in charge of the entire craps pit. The pit boss rarely interacts with players, but he may come over and introduce himself to a high roller and offer her comps.

To play craps, slip into a space by the rail of the table, catch the dealer's attention, give her your cash, and tell her what denomination of chips you'd like. The chips are a great example of casino psychology, by the way. One-dollar chips are called silver, $5 chips are nickels, $25 chips are quarters, and $100 chips are dollars. Doesn't telling your friends back home you lost four bucks sound better than admitting you were a really big loser in Vegas? The player—or shooter—is the one closest to the boxman's left.

When it's your turn to play, the stickman will slide five or six dice to you. Pick two. Your first throw is called the come-out roll, and it's the crucial toss of the game. Make sure the dice make it across the table and bounce off the far end. If you don't, you'll look like a simp, and you'll have to throw them again. This rule is enforced because some cheaters can manipulate dice that don't bounce off the side of the table. When you're the shooter, you're required to make one of two bets: pass or don't pass. "Pass" means you're betting you'll roll a seven or eleven on your come-out roll or that you'll set a point and hit it. "Don't pass" means you don't think you'll roll a seven or eleven. These are called "line bets."

If you do throw a seven or eleven on your come-out roll, it's an automatic winner for you if you've bet on the pass line. Any players who bet on the pass line—called right bettors—also win. If you roll a craps—a two, three, or twelve—then right bettors lose. But anyone who's bet on the don't pass line—called wrong bettors—will win. Sometimes it pays to have a half-empty glass. Automatic winners will have bets paid off or collected. The next roll will be a new come-out roll.

Any other number thrown on the come-out roll—four, five, six, eight, nine, or ten—becomes the point. You'll continue until you repeat your point or throw a seven (called sevening-out). Once a point is established, players betting on the pass and don't pass line will be affected only when the shooter sevens-out or repeats the point. Players have many bets beyond pass and don't pass at their fingertips, which will be discussed later. If you crap out—throw a two, three, or twelve—on your first roll, don't worry. You can shoot again. You don't have to give up the dice until you make a point and then seven-out.

43: THIS CRAPS DOESN'T SUCK: THE BEST CRAPS BETS

The number of bets available at the craps table can make even an experienced player's head swim. But don't fret. Only a few bets are advantageous to players: pass, don't pass, come, don't come, and free-odds bets.

If you bet on the pass line, you're an optimist. You're betting that the shooter will roll a seven or eleven—an automatic winner—or that she will establish and then make her point. For example, let's say she rolls a five with her first throw. That becomes her point. Her second toss is a two. If this were her come-out roll, she'd lose. But since the point has been established, the two is a neutral roll. The shooter then throws a four—another neutral throw. Finally, on her fourth throw, she makes her point and rolls another five. Pass line—or right—bettors win! The payoff for the pass bet is even money, and the house edge for this bet is a low 1.4 percent.

There's a bet for the gloom-and-doomers out there as well, the don't pass—or back-line—bet. These so-called wrong bettors wager that the shooter will roll a two or three—or crap out—on his come-out roll or seven-out before hitting her point. If the shooter throws a twelve, it's a push. The house edge for the don't pass bet is also 1.4 percent.

Come bets are pass bets part deux. The difference is you don't place a come bet until after a point is established. If the shooter rolls a two, three, twelve, seven, or eleven, you can't place a come (or don't come) bet. You can make multiple come bets, depending on the shooter's throw. Let's say the shooter rolls a four on his come-out bet. Thus, four becomes the come point. You can make a come bet for it. On his next throw, the shooter rolls a four. You win! If the shooter rolls another number instead, you can place a come bet on it as well. If a shooter is hot, you can stand to win a lot of money on multiple come bets. The don't come is another bet for pessimists. Once the shooter makes a point, it becomes the don't come point. You're wagering the shooter will seven-out before she hits her point. You can make multiple don't come bets.

The best wager in the house—on any game—is free-odds bets at the craps tables. These are called "free-odds" because once made, the house has no advantage over the player. Free-odds bets are piggyback wagers added to pass, don't pass, come, and don't come bets. Let's say you decide to place an odds bet on the pass line. Once a point is made, you can make an additional bet by placing chips behind your original pass line wager. At many casinos, you can make an odds bet greater than your initial wager. If you make your point, you not only win your original pass line bet, you win your odds bet as well. And the best part is: The odds bet pays correct odds. The odds of rolling a four or ten are two to one. The odds of throwing a five or nine are three to two, and the odds of rolling a six or eight are six to five. When backed with a free-odds bet, the overall odds of the pass, don't pass, come, and don't come bets are reduced to less than 1 percent.

44: Don't make a crappy bet: What you should avoid at the craps table

Pass, don't pass, come, don't come, and odds bets. That's really all you need to remember when it comes to the craps table. Does that mean those are the only bets available? Heck, no! It wouldn't be gambling if there weren't some sucker bets at every table.

Place bets are very popular at the craps table, but you should avoid them unless you and lady luck have a thing going. If you must make a place bet, then give the dealer a chip and tell her you want to place the nine (or whatever number). You're wagering the number nine will be rolled before the shooter sevens-out. The payoffs on place bets are nine to five for four or ten, seven to five for five or nine, and seven to six for six or eight. If you decide to make a place bet, be sure to bet $5 for four, ten, five, or nine (because they pay off in multiples of five) or $6 for six or eight (because these pay off in multiples of six). You can make any number of place bets, as long as you stick to four, five, six, eight, nine, or ten. The house advantage for four or ten is 6.67 percent. The advantage for five or nine is 4 percent, and the house edge for six or eight is 1.52 percent.

At the craps table you can also "buy" the Big 6 or Big 8 bets. If you make the Big 6, you're wagering the shooter will roll a six before she sevens-out. If you make the Big 8, you're betting an eight will be rolled before a player sevens-out. These are similar to place bets, but by "buying" the numbers, you get true odds. If you win, the payout is bigger than a place bet. But you also lose more if the shooter doesn't make your chosen point. The house gets a 5 percent commission on buy bets, so you have to bet a significant amount of money to make the payout work for you.

You could be tempted to buy the four or ten. Doing so reduces the house edge on these numbers from 6.67 percent to 4.76 percent. If you win the bet, you get paid two to one instead of the usual nine to five. But you also have to pay the house that 5 percent commission. It's not worth it. And theoretically, you could buy the five, six, eight, or nine as well. But you'd still have to pay the 5 percent commission, and buying these numbers doesn't make the house edge on them lower than 5 percent.

Lay bets are the opposite of buy bets. For these, you're wagering the shooter will seven-out before the points you bet against are rolled. Lay bets also require a 5 percent commission, and the house edge on them ranges from 2.44 percent to 4 percent. Field bets are made on any number in the field box—the two, three, four, nine, ten, eleven, or twelve. The most frequently rolled numbers are five, six, seven, and eight, however. Casinos usually offer higher payouts for twos and twelves, but even with these bonuses, the number of losing combinations always outnumbers the winning ones. The worst of the worst—the bets you should avoid unless you just want to give away your money to a casino rather than a charitable organization—are the proposition, or center bets. They're at the center of the table, and you make them through the stickman, who's positioned behind them. These wagers include betting on any seven, any craps, the two or twelve, the three or eleven, and the craps-eleven. Center bets should be called sucker bets because that's what they are. The house advantage on them can be as high as 16.67 percent.

45: The fine art of streaking...Or, make sure you cover your ass in craps

You can't pretend to be a craps expert your first few times out, so—if you're a guy—suck up the machismo and be willing to admit you don't know something. Didn't someone once say that pride goeth before losing your money by playing craps without knowing what you're doing? It was something like that anyway.

As an absolute beginner don't roll, just watch. You'll be able to discern veteran players pretty quickly. Ask yourself: What do they do? What bets do they make? What bets do they avoid? There's no law that says you can't ask one of these old hands why she does what she does. People LOVE to feel like experts, like wise gurus dispensing information to the masses.

When you first begin to play, stick with the pass, don't pass, come, don't come, and odds bets. If you observe the action for a while, and the table seems cold—in other words, players aren't making their point before sevening-out—then bet on don't pass and don't come. If shooters are on fire, then bet pass and come. Whichever of these initial bets you make, don't forget to play the odds bet as well. These aren't "advertised." Casinos want new players to be blissfully unaware of player-friendly odds bets. So, if a player sets a point and you bet odds, then you've got three wagers on the table—a good start and not too complicated. Once you feel comfortable with these basics, you can start making additional bets.

Something you're likely to notice if you watch any table is that craps moves in streaks. There's no reason a game of chance should appear predictable, but there are more things in heaven and earth, Horatio, than can be dreamt of using legitimate science. If there's a streak—hot or cold—bet on the streak. Follow the trend unless or until a new one is established. Don't try to be psychic and predict new trends.

Finally, remember that craps is fast-paced. In no time at all, you can go through your bankroll, especially if you're making three bets or more per shooter. Set a realistic win and loss limit for yourself, keep an eye on what you wager, and leave the table once you hit either of your self-imposed limits.

46:

No rabbit's feet at the table: Favorite craps superstitions

Since human beings began walking upright, they've created superstitions to combat mysterious forces. And throwing little plastic cubes upon which ride great sums of money is as mysterious as any natural phenomenon. Other games of chance—like keno and bingo—also have their voodoo and mojo moments, but they don't hold a candle to craps.

The number-one no-no is to call out the number seven when you roll them bones. The dice have ears. They hear you and decide to thwart your intentions. And since most players bet on the pass line, you'll really upset everyone if you don't roll a seven on your come-out throw—because once a point is set, a seven is a very bad thing for pass and come bettors.

Don't let a shooter hit you with the dice because you're dangling your hands down toward the table. If the dice hit you and a seven is rolled, you will become the craps goat. Your fellow players will dislike you and besmirch your mother's reputation underneath their collective breath. Make your bets early, and listen for the stickman to signal the shooter is about to roll. Then make sure your fingers are not hanging over the edge of the table.

If you get a little overexcited and your dice bounce off the table, get the same dice. You may be tempted to get new dice, thinking your exuberance unlucky. To other players, though, switching dice is tantamount to changing the entire mechanics of the game. And if your dice have been hot when you switch them, fellow players will whisper even more unpleasant things about your sainted mother.

If you see an empty craps table, avoid it. If you're a beginner, it may be tempting to play alone, in case you make an embarrassing move. But there's usually a reason why a table is being quarantined: It's cold. Playing alone will keep it cold, so the superstition goes. Find a table with lots of action and play there. Veteran players believe lady luck will smile if the dice don't take too many tumbles during their journey to the far side of the table. The more they tumble, superstitious logic goes, the more likely they are to come up seven immediately after a point is established. Another superstition involving the dice's journey involves the mirrors on the inside walls of the table, opposite the dealers. Supposedly, a roll will be more beneficial to all concerned if the dice bounce off of the mirror. Casinos, understandably, prefer you not to destroy their mirrors. Besides, all superstitious folks know that breaking a mirror is one of the worst sins you can commit.

And finally, the oldest craps superstition involves "virgins." Supposedly, if a woman has never thrown dice at a craps table before—in other words, if she is a craps virgin—

she will have a hot streak. The magic doesn't work for virgin guys. Spankin' new guys are considered triple mojo bad luck.

47: THIS ISN'T THE RUSSIAN VARIETY, RIGHT? THE HISTORY OF ROULETTE

Roulette is one of the most popular forms of gambling in Europe, but in the United States it's practically an afterthought. Why? It's mostly because of differences between American and European wheels and rules. The American version of roulette creates a large house edge that makes the game more a diversion than a quick and easy way to strike it rich. The game also isn't as popular because it's the slowest of table games, and Americans are not known for copious reserves of patience. Still, roulette is one of the most visually arresting casino games, with its multicolored chips and striking, number-covered wheel.

Roulette's origins are shrouded in mystery, though it's likely that games of chance involving wheels were invented soon after the wheel itself. The modern version of the game is believed to date back to eighteenth century France. "Roulette" is French for "small wheel." Early wheels had slots for thirty-six numbers plus zero and double zero. These are the wheels you will find today in American casinos. In the mid-nineteenth century, Frenchman Louis Blanc created the single-zero roulette wheel, which improved players' odds. Blanc introduced the new wheel to a gaming hall he owned in Germany, and it spun 'round the clock.

Roulette owes its whiff of sophistication to Germany, which decided to outlaw gambling during the time that roulette became a popular pastime. Blanc convinced royalty in the tiny country of Monaco to allow him to open a casino there. Then he managed to talk the French government into providing a rail line to the country. *Voila*! Monaco became the world's premier gambling spot, and it was the only place anybody could—legally—play roulette in Europe until the 1930s. The world's wealthiest people flocked to Monaco in their tuxedos and evening gowns.

The original, double-zero version of roulette began to make its way into America's frontier towns in the nineteenth century. Single-zero roulette has never caught on in this country, probably because it favors players and not the house. There are many available bets at the roulette table, but it's simple to make them. There's no foolproof strategy for roulette because it's a game of chance, not skill. And it's slow. Three hands of blackjack can take place during one spell of betting and spinning at the roulette table. The slow pace of roulette makes the game a fun one for cutting your gambling teeth. The play is leisurely, and you can feel—just for a little while—like you're living the lavish lifestyle of the rich and famous . . . even if you're wearing Bermuda shorts and knee socks instead of a tuxedo.

48: ROUND AND ROUND SHE GOES: THE BASICS OF ROULETTE PLAY

No game in the casino offers more individual bets than roulette, from bets for even money to those that can win you 35 times your wager. Fortunes can be won or lost on one spin of the wheel. The variety of bets, the whiff of sophistication roulette expels, and the ease of its basic rules make roulette an exciting game for beginners and old pros alike.

Roulette is played with a circular wheel containing thirty-eight numbered, grooved slots. The numbers are one through thirty-six, zero, and double zero. Half the primary numbers are black, the other half red. Zeros are green. To one side of the wheel is a betting layout offering a smorgasbord of choices: spots for each individual primary number which are divided into three long columns and twelve short ones, one for zero, one for double zero, one marked one to eighteen, one marked nineteen to thirty-six, one marked odd, one marked even, one for black, one for red, one for all numbers from one to twelve, one for all numbers from thirteen to twenty-four, one for all numbers from twenty-five to thirty-six, and three for column bets—bets made for any number that falls within one of the three long columns.

Once you place your bets, the dealer—or croupier—will spin the roulette wheel and then throw a little metal ball onto it so that it travels in the opposite direction. If you're struck with divine inspiration after the wheel is already spinning, you still have time to make a bet. But once the wheel begins to slow, the dealer will say something like, "No more bets" or "Fuhgeddaboudit."

At roulette tables, you'll get special chips—or wheel checks—that help the croupier keep up with which chips belong to which players. Chips can be any value you tell the dealer you want them to be—as long as the value doesn't surpass the table maximum. The dealer will put a marker with your amount on top of your color chip at the outer edge of the wheel. After the wheel has stopped and the ball falls into its chosen slot, the dealer will swipe losing bets off the table and pay winners. The total combination of bets is 150, and you can place as many as you like—as long as the total doesn't surpass the table maximum. There are two basic kinds of bets: inside and outside. Inside bets involve the spaces that include numbers, and outside bets use the other spaces— those outside the numbers.

There are a variety of inside bets. The straight bet involves placing a wager on a single number. If you place one and win, your return is a whopping thirty-five to one. The split bet involves placing your chip on a line between two numbers. Split bets pay out at seventeen to one. The trio bet involves any of the twelve short columns. The payout of the trio bet is eleven to one. For a four-number bet, place a wheel check at the spot that marks the intersection of four numbers. If the ball lands on any of these numbers, the payout is eight to one. The five-number bet involves only zero, double zero, one, two, and three. Place a chip at the intersection of these five numbers to make your wager, then pray with zealous fervor. If you hit, the payout is six to one. The final inside bet is the six-number—or block—bet. It's similar to a trio bet, only you place a chip or chips on the outside line between two three-column sets of numbers. Block bets pay out at five to one.

Roulette also offers a number of outside bets. For a columns bet, place your chip or chips on one of the boxes marked 2 to 1 at the bottom of one of the long columns. You get two to one if you hit any of the numbers in that column. Another way to bet twelve numbers is the dozens bet. Place your wheel checks on one or more of the boxes marked 1st 12, 2nd 12, or 3rd 12. This bet also pays two to one. And finally, there are a few even-money outside bets. One of these is red-black. Place your wager on the box marked red or black. Another even bet is high-low. For this bet, place a chip on the box marked 1 to 18 or 19 to 36. The final even-money bet is odd-even. For this bet, place a chip or chips on the even or odd rectangle.

49: This wheel's on fire: The art of charting

Roulette is the only table game in a casino that can suffer from mechanical glitches. A roulette wheel can be "biased," meaning it can have a flaw that causes it to favor one number—or a set of adjacent numbers—over other spots on the wheel. You may not find a wheel in the casino that appears biased, but it's worth taking the time to scout around for one. Why? Because roulette odds are horrible. The house advantage for most bets is 5.26 percent. And it's even higher for the five-number bet: a whopping 7.29 percent.

To find a biased wheel, watch a particular wheel to see if a certain number shows up often. What's "often"? On average, a number will only come up one out of every thirty-eight spins. At many casinos, roulette tables feature a digital display showing the result of the last twenty or so spins. Casinos don't mind "helping" you chart because in-house charting is another of those Pavlovian devices that are irresistible attractions to gamblers. Chances are if the digital display is at one table and not at another, the one with the numbers will see steady action. But here's the rub: Twenty spins won't tell you a damn thing. It takes hundreds of spins before you can tell if a wheel is biased. And even if you don't want to watch a wheel spin that many times, you need to observe it over a period of days or at least over several hours. Twenty spins are a come-on to attract newcomers and not really a player-friendly act of assistance.

If you find a wheel that appears to have a bias, then put your wheel checks on the proper number or numbers. Play for thirty-eight spins, one for each number on the wheel. If you're winning money after thirty-eight spins, keep your initial bankroll plus 50 percent of your winnings. Start over with what's left.

Charting has many drawbacks for the casual gambler. It requires an inordinate amount of patience, something lacking even in a building without clocks. And it requires a big investment, not to mention a degree of luck. But if you truly have found a biased wheel, the result can be a boon to your bankroll. If patience and mucho moolah are not at your disposal, however, then focus instead on the column strategy.

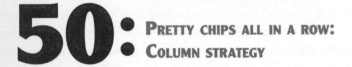 **50:** Pretty chips all in a row: Column strategy

Herculean amounts of patience are required when charting a roulette wheel to check for bias. But the column strategy increases your chances of winning without having to devote hours of study to individual wheels. It's a strategy that lets you be somewhat impulsive while playing smart. Column strategy is also called dozens strategy because it utilizes the bet boxes on the table that involve sets of twelve numbers. You can bet on the first, second, and third sets of twelve numbers, or you can bet on the three long columns. Both bets pay off two to one.

Let's say you decide to use the first, second, and third sets, and you've elected to make your wheel checks worth $5 apiece. Place your bet on two of the three sets, say the first and third. Now you've got all but twelve of the primary numbers covered. If a number in the first set comes up, then you're ahead by $5. On the next spin, add another chip to the first column of twelve numbers and also play the second column. Don't bet on the third this time. If a number from the first column comes up again, then you're up by $15. On the next bet, add another $5 to the first column, and switch back to a bet on the third column. Don't bet on the second set of twelve this time. Always increase your bet on the winning column and switch your other bet before every spin. If you win two times in a row on the same column, then you're gambling with the house's money.

If you get on a streak and win the equivalent of at least a quarter of your bankroll, then take a chance on throwing a bit of charting into your play. Even if you don't have the patience to watch a wheel spin hundreds of times, you may find that a particular series of adjacent numbers has been popping up more than pure physics should allow. Put a wager on a number or two—using the house's money—and you could go from being a winner to being a WINNER. For that matter, you can make any other additional bet you might like from time to time—a split, a trio, or a block bet, for example.

With columns strategy, you're covering a maximum amount of numbers with minimum bets. If you hit one of your two bets, you'll come out ahead, even though you lose the other bet. The columns strategy takes into account two-thirds of the numbers on the table—not counting the zeros—and this makes for pretty good odds . . . for roulette. Over time the house advantage is bound to make you a loser. But roulette can be a fun, social game. Once you've decided on a particular strategy or set of "lucky" numbers, you can turn off your brain, relax, and see if luck is on your side before heading off to one of those infernal games that actually makes you think.

51: How about a European vacation? Look for "European" roulette wheels

The United States is a rarity in the world of roulette. As explained in the previous points, while most countries have a single zero on their wheels, American wheels have a double zero as well. The original wheels, invented in Europe, had zero and double zero. But Europeans also developed the single-zero wheel. It's probably one reason that Europeans consider Americans so gauche and unsophisticated. We still have two numbers on our roulette wheels that make most players' bets null and void. This house edge in domestic casinos makes the game a bad choice for gamblers interested more in winning money than in gambling for fun and diversion. Not only do European wheels have the single zero, they also have rules that favor gamblers. American roulette has a house advantage ranging from a dismal 5.26 percent to a truly sucky 7.29 percent.

By contrast, European roulette has a casino edge of only 1.35 percent. If you can find an American casino advertising European roulette, then run—don't walk—to that table. Stay away from American roulette if you can. Be really smart and use this incontrovertible fact to convince your significant other that a trip to Europe would be a really great value. From the get-go, the single zero on European wheels drops the casino's edge to 2.7 percent, and it eliminates the five-number bet, which offers the worst odds of the game on American wheels. European roulette also features two rules that are extremely beneficial to players: en prison and partage. With the inclusion of these rules, the house edge in Europe is decreased to less than 1.5 percent.

Under American rules, you lose if the ball lands on zero or double zero and you haven't bet on one of them. In Europe, if the ball lands on zero, the en prison rule comes into effect. You either surrender half your bet—partage—or "imprison" your bet for another spin—en prison. If you elect to leave your bet en prison and you win the spin, you're free to take that wager and do with it what you will. Chances are you won't find European wheels or rules in Las Vegas casinos. Atlantic City resorts offer partage, though they call it "surrender," presumably to distance themselves from the taint of all things French.

What Are the Odds? . . .
What You Didn't Know
about Vegas Shows

You'll notice that Las Vegas isn't called the Gambling Capital of the World, even though it probably is. It's the Entertainment Capital of the World. Many of those who have graced the city's stages have been legitimate kings and queens of entertainment. But Las Vegas is also the city where entertainers you thought were dead still play two shows a night for a two-drink minimum.

Sometimes the city has been the last resort for has-beens, which is what Ronald Regan had become by the time he took the stage at the Last Frontier. At one time, he was Warner Brothers' top draw, but by the 1950s, work was scarce for the actor. After his stint in Vegas, Reagan turned to television and later, a successful political career.

Las Vegas has also been a magnet for offbeat acts. One of those was Christine Jorgensen, at one time our nation's most famous transgendered performer. The former George Jorgensen was a top draw on the Strip, who often lampooned her controversy by singing songs like "I Enjoy Being a Girl." She may well have been the precursor to today's popular Vegas shows that feature wisecracking transvestites.

During this lounge act, you'll also learn about the disastrous first engagement of a young man named Elvis Presley, who later went on to some degree of fame in Sin City. And you'll spend a little time with those loveable lads from Liverpool, The Beatles, who played Las Vegas during the band's first full-scale American concert tour. The shows got a lukewarm response, just like the King's earliest performances, which may explain why the group never again played the Entertainment Capital of the World.

Finally, we'll learn about the days when Las Vegas shows were practically given away. In the days of Mafia control, mobsters treated shows and restaurants as gravy. Casinos were the prime rib. Once corporations took over the city, everything became prime rib.

52: THE GREAT COMMUNICATOR CRACKS WISE: RONALD REAGAN LIVE AT THE LAST FRONTIER

It shouldn't be too surprising that fortieth president Ronald Reagan did a two-week stint as part of a comedy team that performed at the Last Frontier, one of the first casinos built on the Strip. After all, the Great Communicator was known for his wit. Sometimes it showed strength, as when he quipped to his wife Nancy that he "forgot to duck" out of the way of bullets John Hinckley, Jr. fired. Sometimes the cracks got him into trouble, like when he told an open microphone that the United States had banned the Soviet Union, and "we begin bombing in five minutes." And hey, don't forget that flair for comedy he demonstrated as second banana to a chimp in *Bedtime for Bonzo* nor that hilarious misunderstanding called the Iran-Contra Affair. But when Reagan took the stage at the Last Frontier, it was no laughing matter—it was a last resort.

Reagan began his entertainment career as an announcer at radio station WOC in Davenport, Iowa. He was clever enough to use his sportscasting career as a springboard to Hollywood. Reagan talked his station manager into letting him shadow Chicago's major league baseball teams in the midst of their spring training—in California. Through an acquaintance who was a burgeoning starlet for RKO, Reagan later got a screen test with Warner Bros. He did a brief scene with the actress Helen Valkis and was sure he'd totally blown it. Reagan went back to radio, convinced he'd lost his chance at the big leagues. Days later, a telegram arrived, offering Reagan a seven-year contract at Warner Bros., starting at $200 a week.

Reagan's first film was 1937's *Love Is on the Air*, in which he played a roving radio reporter who gets embroiled in crime-fighting. He got good reviews and soon became one of Warner's most dependable stars, though most of his work was in B pictures like *Sergeant Murphy* and *Accidents Will Happen*. Once Reagan became involved with and married Jane Wyman, the two became one of Hollywood's favorite power couples. For a while, Reagan was Hollywood's number-one box office draw, and he became president of the Screen Actors Guild. As the 1940s progressed, Reagan's star began to descend as Wyman's rose higher and higher. The two divorced in 1948. By 1954, Reagan was a has-been. But he had a new family with Nancy Davis, and he needed work.

Like a lot of has-beens, almost-rans and never-quites, Reagan turned to Las Vegas. On February 15, 1954, he began a two-week stint at the Last Frontier as emcee for The Continentals, a sort of sub-bargain-basement Marx Brothers. Reagan told Irish jokes, put on a German accent, acted drunk, and generally horsed around. But mostly, he played straight man to the zany antics of The Continentals. Reagan was a good sport, but as he stood up there on the small stage of the Ramona Room, he must have thought he'd hit the entertainment skids. As she always did, Nancy was there by his side to cheer on her Ronnie.

Reagan was a hit. If there's one thing Reagan could do—as actor, governor, and president—it was command an audience. The Continentals featuring Ronald Reagan was a sell-out smash. Reagan received regular standing ovations—and an offer to extend his engagement. He was offered more money and a chance to perform at New York hotspots, but Reagan turned it down. Soon after his short-lived time as a Vegas headliner, Reagan became a spokesman for General Electric and host of *General Electric Theater*. He parlayed his experience as a spokesman and as president of SAG into a career in politics.

53: The Atomic-Powered Singer bombs: Elvis's first appearance in Las Vegas

Even nonfans of Elvis Presley know a few things about him: He's the King of Rock 'n' Roll. He really, really, really loved his mama. He made a bunch of bad films. And he is synonymous with Las Vegas.

What we think about when we think about Elvis is usually a rhinestone-clad, cape-wearing, scarf-throwing—maybe a little overweight—king holding court over crowds at the International Hotel, later the Las Vegas Hilton.

It's true Elvis was a smash when he began his exclusive engagement at the International on July 31, 1969. He was fresh from his so-called '68 Comeback Special and beginning his second—and unfortunately final—career revival (the first revival, by the way, was after he got out of the Army). By the end of the concerts on August 28, he had played to more than 100,000 enthusiastic fans, and his shows had grossed more than $1.5 million.

He returned several times to Las Vegas after that triumphant performance. For much of the 1970s, Elvis was more than just the King of Rock 'n' Roll. He was also the King of the Las Vegas Strip. A life-size statue of the performer remains inside the Las Vegas Hilton. But Elvis didn't play Las Vegas for the first time in 1969, and his first engagement was far from a triumph.

Elvis first came to Sin City for an engagement at the recently renamed New Frontier Hotel (someone must have decided that the Last Frontier sounded too grim). It began on April 23, 1956, and was to end four weeks later. At that time, Elvis was called the Hillbilly Cat or the Atomic-Powered Singer. In a town where visitors entertained themselves by watching mushroom clouds emerge from nearby above-ground nuclear tests, the Atomic-Powered Singer seemed a sure bet.

Besides, he had the number one song in the country: "Heartbreak Hotel." He was mobbed by young girls wherever he played. No one actually could hear Elvis perform in concert because those same young girls screamed at the top of their lungs during entire shows.

But in the Entertainment Capital of the World, the Atomic-Powered Singer bombed . . . big time. The older, middle-American audience damned Elvis with faint praise. Instead of nonstop screaming, he got polite—and short-lived—applause. If anyone wanted to mob him, it was because he or she was so irritated by his performance.

Within days of his first show, Elvis was bumped from the top-billed spot on the New Frontier's marquee. He was a distant third, underneath Shecky Greene and the Freddie Martin Band. Elvis's four-week stint ended early, on May 6.

Recordings of that final night at the New Frontier exist and can be found on the fifth disc of *The Complete 50's Masters* box set. For even casual fans, the recordings are eerie. An obviously uncomfortable Elvis calls the Heartbreak Hotel the "Heartburn Motel" in one verse of his hit song. His between-song patter might as well be accompanied by the sound of chirping crickets. He refers to his "little" songs that can be found on his "little" records. In 1956, Las Vegas just wasn't ready for Elvis Presley. But thirteen years later, the King of Rock 'n' Roll came back, his crown firmly intact, his fans suitably exuberant.

54: PRESENTING THE FORMER GEORGE JORGENSEN: CHRISTINE JORGENSEN PLAYS THE DUNES POST-OP

Transgendered people are folks who feel strongly they are women in men's bodies or men in women's bodies. These days, most people accept that the condition exists, but on December 1, 1952, this headline shocked the world: "Ex-GI Becomes Blonde Bombshell."

George Jorgensen didn't intend to become the center of a media circus when he went to Copenhagen for a series of operations that transformed the Army veteran into Christine Jorgensen. But word of his operations leaked to the press, and he—and then she—became the most written about figure of 1953, the same year *Playboy Magazine* was launched. The Bronx photographer had known since childhood that he should have been born a she. And even though Europe pioneered sex-change operations in the 1930s, Jorgensen's act of changing his sex was revolutionary and extremely controversial in America, during the early days of the Eisenhower administration.

When Jorgensen deplaned at Idlewild Airport on February 12, 1953, she was an instant celebrity. And she was the instant butt of comedians's jokes, who called her "man's gift to women" and "tops in swaps." Jorgensen took all of the ribbing and controversy in stride. She became the subject of gossipy articles and was an inspiration for Ed Wood's first completed film, 1953's *Glen or Glenda?* (Wood went on to direct the so-called worst film ever made, *Plan 9 from Outer Space.*) In fact, throughout the 1950s and early 1960s, she parlayed the controversy surrounding her into a successful entertainment career that took her to theaters throughout the world, from Europe to Havana to Hollywood to the world's entertainment capital.

Jorgensen usually performed at either the Sahara or the Dunes. A table placard from one of her Dunes' appearances proclaims her "the most controversial figure in show business today" and insists that if you haven't seen her live, you don't really know Christine Jorgensen—no matter how many lurid media accounts you've read. "She is probably one of the most charming feminine entertainers in show business," the placard proclaims, adding that "Miss Jorgensen holds an all-time attendance record at the Sahara Hotel in Las Vegas."

Jorgensen semiretired from show business in the mid-1960s, settling first in Long Island, later in Los Angeles's infamous Chateau Marmont (site of comedian John Belushi's overdose), and finally in San Clemente. In 1987, she was diagnosed with bladder cancer. Jorgensen died two years later at the age of sixty-two.

55: 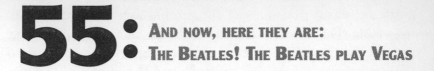 AND NOW, HERE THEY ARE: THE BEATLES! THE BEATLES PLAY VEGAS

By 1964, the four lads from Liverpool were already the subject of Beatlemania on their side of the big pond. The Beatles had their first British number one—with "Please Please Me"—in February of 1963. After that, there was no looking back. But in America, attempts to duplicate that success failed at first. Early in 1964, "I Want to Hold Your Hand" suddenly caught fire in the land of Cadillacs, Howard Hughes, and Elvis Presley. Pop historians tend to "credit" the assassination of John F. Kennedy with The Beatles' success. After those bleak days of round-the-clock television coverage, Americans—especially young ones—were ready for something brighter.

The group arrived in the United States for the first time on February 7, 1964. When they touched down at New York's recently renamed Kennedy Airport, they found themselves in the midst of Beatlemania in full bloom. Two days later, the lads played *The Ed Sullivan Show* for the first time, to an audience of 73 million. The group's first concert was in Washington, D.C. But the group's first full-fledged American tour began on August 19, at San Francisco's Cow Palace. Stop two was the Las Vegas Convention Center.

The Sahara Hotel and Casino sponsored the Beatles, despite the fact that most of the group's fans were too young to gamble. The Beatles flew to Las Vegas moments after their show at the Cow Palace, arriving in the Entertainment Capital of the World at 1 A.M. The group played two shows on August 20—one at 4 P.M. and one at 9 P.M. In between, the loveable moptops found time to pose for photos and gamble a bit.

At the shows, The Beatles played "I Want to Hold Your Hand," "Twist and Shout," "She Loves You," and "All My Loving," among other classics. The combined total for the shows was 16,000 fans. Not bad, but not as many seats as the group filled for one show in San Francisco. Las Vegas was still a pretty small town then, and The Beatles ran into the same problem as their hero Elvis did during his first Vegas engagement. Sin City just wasn't ready yet for something as exotic as The Beatles in 1964, any more than it had been hep to something as exotic as Elvis in 1956.

The Beatles officially broke up in 1970. If, like Elvis, they'd given Las Vegas another try around that time, it's a safe bet the Fab Four would have gotten a reception fit for The King.

56: **Those priceless good old days: Steak dinners and the Rat Pack for less than ten bucks**

Once upon a time, only the slot machines and table games in Las Vegas took your money. Entertainment and fine dining were dirt-cheap. And while you can still find good deals on buffets—which are more like pastures for human beings than fine dining—you'll be hard-pressed to find affordable entertainment featuring big names. Sure, you can attend Dick Furtado's World of Mystical, Magical Illusory Illusions for a two-drink minimum. But semipermanent shows by the likes of *Titanic* chanteuse Celine Dion and Cirque du Soleil will set you back around $100 apiece. During Vegas's glory days, the ones that still serve as the bedrock of Sin City's appeal, the situation couldn't have been more different.

In his excellent book, *Fly on the Wall: Recollection of Las Vegas' Good Old Bad Old Days*, former journalist and casino marketing director Dick Odessky describes the "Good Old Prices" of the city's past. In the famous Copa Room, showplace of the Sands, you and a date could have cocktails, a lavish steak dinner, and take in a show for less than $10. And it wasn't just any show. It likely began with beautiful chorus girls wearing costumes and headdresses that staggered the imagination. They were followed by a well-known comedian. And then the headliners would take the stage. You could have seen Frank, Dean, Sammy, Peter, and Joey. Maybe rub shoulders with some of their Hollywood buddies—or their friend Sen. John F. Kennedy—and get change for a ten-spot. Even adjusted for inflation, that was a helluva deal.

In the early 1960s, you could also have first-class accommodations on the Strip for $5 a night. The Tropicana was, in those days, Las Vegas's most lavish hotel, offering top amenities and marketing itself to high rollers. Even there, rooms were only $14 a night. And then there were those famous "chuckwagon dinners," the precursors to today's buffets. Chuckwagons offered sumptuous spreads with prime rib sliced to order, fresh shrimp and crab, caviar, and desserts that were meals in themselves. The cost for all of this was around a dollar, maybe as much as a buck and a quarter.

Why were prices so low? Casino properties didn't mind taking a loss on their rooms, food, and entertainment. If all of these amenities were cheap, then they would entice folks inside. And—just like today—you couldn't get to the dining hall or the showroom without walking past all of that hot action in the casino. If you ate like a pig and then laughed yourself thin again thanks to the antics of the Rat Pack, you probably felt like a million bucks. Maybe if you tried your luck at the craps table, the thinking went, you'd leave feeling like two million bucks.

Las Vegas gambling profits topped $110 million in 1960. Casinos weren't really giving away something for nothing. They just treated everything but the slots and tables as gravy. Tourists today have Howard Hughes to thank for the end of the good old prices and the advent of the rotten new ones. Hughes managed to convince the state to license corporations, and he did his convincing without ever being seen in public. Prior to Hughes, only individuals could get gambling licenses. Corporations? No way. The state would have had to license each individual shareholder. But as he so often did, Hughes changed the rules.

Once corporations, such as major chain hotels, began to run casino properties, bigwigs were shocked at how much previous hotel management had practically given away. Corporations decided that rooms, food, and entertainment needed to be money-makers, not gravy. Nowadays, it's the casino's profits that are the icing on the cake. The days when those profits WERE the cake are long gone. By the close of the 1960s, $10 rooms were $25 rooms. Chuckwagon dinners were gone, replaced by $1.95 breakfast buffets. Caviar was nowhere in sight. Dinners were $20 a plate, not $10 per couple. And the new stars of the Strip demanded—and received—much more than ten bucks. Siegfried & Roy, for example, started out as the closing act in the Stardust's *Lido de Paris* show, when the spectacle cost less than $25 per couple. By the close of the twentieth century, the lion-taming magician duo charged $90 per person. Sure, in its "good old days" the Mafia ran Las Vegas. But mobsters only stole from each other, not from the guests staying and playing in their hotels.

PART 4:

BANDITS AND ONSCREEN JOKERS: SLOTS AND VIDEO POKER

SLOTS ARE HOT. God, people love 'em. It doesn't matter that the house edge on slot machines is ridiculously high. What matters is that they're so easy to play, and you could just be one of those lucky schlubs who picks the right machine and wins the jackpot of a lifetime. Goodbye, Waukesha. Hello, Tahiti! Goodbye, Marge. Hello, Leilani!

The appeal of winning life-altering sums of money is obvious. But the machines themselves also have a mysterious allure. They're rife with mysterious symbols. They're colorful, loud, and wild. Some of them even pay homage to favorite pieces of popular culture: Elvis, *Wheel of Fortune*, *Sesame Street*. OK, I don't think there's a *Sesame Street* slot machine . . . at least not yet. Maybe by the time this book goes to press . . .

In this section, you'll find out how slots began. They're a uniquely American device, which may also be part of their appeal. Baccarat and roulette carry the taint of snooty European couture, but slots are the equivalent of Pabst Blue Ribbon and "I'm with Stupid" T-shirts. Then you'll learn why it's important to join a casino's slot club, before turning to strategies that could increase your chances of hitting some jackpots.

Then you'll get the low-down on video poker, another popular form of Man versus Machine gambling. You'll find out about a cheap way to become a pro at the game and how to find machines with the best odds. And finally, you'll learn some tips for giving yourself the best opportunities to win the big, big money at video poker.

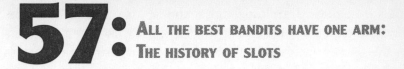

57: All the best bandits have one arm: The history of slots

Slot machines are irresistible magnets for your spare change. They are the most popular way to gamble. Why? Well, for one thing, they're everywhere. If you're in Las Vegas, you don't have to go to Caesars Palace to play slots. You can play moments after you get off the plane, since they're in the airport. They're at the convenience store where you pump gas into your rental car. They're at the supermarket. They're at Wal-Mart. They're in bars. They're in nursery schools and daycare centers. Okay, okay, they're not really in daycare centers and nursery schools . . . at least not yet.

Slots are also popular because they're designed to be as tantalizing as possible. It's easy to forget that the average house edge for slot machines is around 15 percent. And—let's get metaphysical here—maybe slots are so popular because they speak to the American collective unconscious. They're one of the few games in a casino invented in this country, and they hark back to the heady days of the industrial age, when the United States began its ascent to world superpower.

Slot machines were invented in the 1890s by a Bavarian immigrant named Charles Fey, who worked as a machinist. His basic design is still in use. He created a boxy device with a handle that housed three wheels bearing different symbols: hearts, spades, diamonds, horseshoes, stars, Liberty Bells. Payouts depended on lining up three of the same symbols on the same row, visible through a window on the machine's face. The biggest payout on these early machines came from lining up the Liberty Bells, so the slots became known as "Liberty Bell slots" or "Bells."

Fey put his machines in bars all over San Francisco, and they were a big hit from the start. At first, payouts came in the form of free drinks. But money quickly became the payout of choice. These early slots used nickels, at a time when a nickel actually was worth something. If you lined up three bells, you'd get a huge payout: ten nickels. In those days, 50 cents could get you dinner at a fine restaurant with enough left over for a show. Fey split the profits with bar owners. It didn't take long for other folks to build slots, some of them offering modifications that are still in use.

Around the turn of the century, Herbert Stephen Mills widened the payout window so the rows above and below the payoff line were visible. This is one of the features that make slots so addictive. You've put in your money. The wheels spin. And there on the payout line you've got . . . nothing. But look! Look! Right there above the payout line, all three jackpot symbols are lined up. Holy crap, you're THIS CLOSE to easy street! Surely the symbols will be on the payout line on the next spin!

And why are you so eager to see those symbols line up? Because of another one of Mills's innovations: the jackpot.

You could win a hundred nickels, rather than just ten. The booty was in plain sight, behind a window in the center of the machine. If you lined up the right symbols, then everything inside that window dropped out of the machine and into your coffers. Mills also created an innovation that made the likelihood of these massive payouts little more than a delightful pipe dream. He increased the size of the wheels, adding more symbols and making the big payout at best a remote possibility. Mills' machines had twenty symbols total on the wheels, and only one jackpot symbol on each wheel, making the odds of hitting the jackpot one in 8,000.

The odds of hitting mega-jackpots are even worse, but that doesn't stop people from trying their luck. Subsequent innovations to slots have made them sophisticated computers with absolute control over all payouts. Modern slots also allow for multiple coins, which can increase the jackpot when additional coins are used. And machines today offer buttons in addition to or instead of the handle, so that all you have to do to wager your next bet is push a button marked "play max bet." This is America. Who needs to exercise? Fey's invention has changed significantly over the years, but the basic principle is the same: Slot machines offer the illusion of winning something—a big something—for almost nothing.

58: HOW TO BE A "PLAYA": USE THAT SLOT CARD

Comps are one of gambling's glories—what's better than free stuff the house gives you? Of course, it's free like "buy six get one free" is free. You don't get stuff gratis without spending a lot of money first. At card and table games, comps typically go only to big winners. That's because comps are fancy carrots dangled off of spangly sticks. The rewards usually are free nights in the hotel, free dinner at one of the casino's restaurants, or tickets to one of the property's shows. Do you see the pattern? Each reward gets you to return to the property after you've left the tables with a fat wallet. Since the odds always favor the house, odds are when you return for that free steak and decide to add to your windfall, you'll lose your shirt instead.

Slot machines offer a unique form of comps: the slot club card. Notice that the card makes you a member of a club. You *belong*. You're not just someone idly pulling handles and sipping mai tais while the grandkids spend their own quarters in the arcade. No, you have a player's card. YOU ARE A PLA-YA. One of the elite.

So, before you drop anything into a one-armed bandit, find the customer service booth at the casino and ask if the place has a slot club. The larger casinos usually have them. If the casino does have a slot club, then an employee will hand you a form to fill out with some basic information. Casinos use the cards to track your play. If you play often, then a property might keep track of your birthday by using the information from the card. Don't expect a diamond ring in the mail or anything, but you might get a coupon for a free dinner.

Once you've handed in the form, you'll get a card that resembles an ATM or credit card—other cards that assist you in parting with your money. You may also get a clip with a long plastic string attached. This is to keep up with your card, since the tendency can be—if you don't play often—to leave your card in the slot machine when you're done playing. Attach one end of the plastic chain to your belt loop or other suitable object on your person, and then the other end connects to the slot card. Admittedly, more women than men use these chains. It's just not macho to be attached to a slot machine by a lemon yellow or bubble gum-pink piece of stretchy plastic.

Once you have your slot card, put it into the slot machine before you start to play. When you put in the card, a display will say something like, "Welcome back to (state casino name here) Joe Blow." Then as you play, you'll notice you accrue points. Points are racked up not by how many times you pull the handle, but by how much money you play. In other words, don't think that you can earn more free stuff by dividing your $20 kitty into eighty individual, single-quarter games.

Generally speaking, you get a point for every unit played in the slot machine: For instance, if it's a quarter slot, then you get a point for each quarter you put into the machine. And remember, once you start playing, you'll win some pulls. When you play with that money, you also get points. So, if you play with five bucks and get a few minor jackpots, you may end up penniless. But if you're part of the slot club, then at least you've got points to show for your trouble.

If you graduated to casinos from arcades you'll be familiar with how slot cards work. Remember how you played Skeeball, and a certain amount of points netted you tickets for "valuable" prizes like erasers in the shape of lips or a piece of penny candy you got by spending a quarter? Slot clubs work the same way. The more money you put into a slot machine, the more points you accrue. Casinos with slot clubs usually have signs that trumpet the rewards of their slot club. Get a polyester hat with our logo on it for just fifty points!—that sort of thing.

When you feel you've earned enough points for the comp of your choice, take the card to customer service and cash it in. Then you're free to go out and start racking up more points. You should check out the rewards offered by various casinos. The slot club rewards loyalty since you won't earn points on, say, a Harrah's card if you're playing at Caesars. Oh, and guys, don't forget to remove the slot card after you've played. Aw heck—just bite the bullet and proudly attach yourself to the machine with that lime green chain. It doesn't make you any less of a man.

59: REACH FOR THE SKY: SLOTS WITH THE BEST ODDS

Slot machines are popular because they are easy to play and give you that pulse-quickening thrill every time you pull the handle. Like all the games in a casino, slots use psychology to keep you coming back for more—perhaps you'll get THIS CLOSE to a triple-bar jackpot. Or you might get a small pay-out—enough to make you feel you're winning something but not enough to make you quit trying for more. Or you'll be next to some lucky schlub who's hit a big jackpot. As those coins tumble loudly next to you, just try and keep yourself from pulling a handle of your own.

Unfortunately, there are only two ways to increase your odds for winning at slot machines. One is luck. The other is to play machines with higher denominations. Five-dollar slots have better odds than dollar slots, which have better odds than half-dollar slots, which have better odds than quarter slots, and so on. Therein lies the rub.

If you're playing slots just to kill time before the latest former Broadway star takes the stage for a Las Vegas spectacle, then you could lose an awful lot on a $5 slot in fifteen minutes. On average, for an hour of play, you would bet $30 on nickel slots for a one-coin bet; $60 for a two-coin bet; and $90 for a three-coin bet. Move up to a quarter slot, then you'd play $150 in an hour for a one-coin bet; $300 for a two-coin bet; and $450 for a three-coin bet. On a dollar slot, you can put away $600 an hour for a one-coin bet; $1,200 for a two-coin bet; and $1,800 for a three-coin bet. And on a $5 slot? You could play a hefty $3,000 for a one-coin bet in an hour; $6,000 for a two-coin bet; and $9,000 for a three-coin bet. Chances are, you'll get some good payouts on that $5 slot in an hour, but there's no guarantee you'll come out ahead. Slot machines can cost you a lot of money very quickly, and the odds of a jackpot are in the vicinity of one in 8,000.

But wait, you say, casinos are filled with signs that say, "Our slots have a 99 percent payout rate!" That's true—sort of. First of all, even if a machine has a 99 percent payout rate, it doesn't mean that you'll lose only 1 percent of your gambling money. It means that over time, the machine will pay back 99 percent. Therefore, you might play for an hour and lose $1,200, only to watch the next player walk up, put in $3 and win the maximum jackpot. Hey, it's called gambling. There are no sure shots.

The other problem with "99 percent payouts" is that, while the claim most likely is true, it doesn't mean that EVERY slot in the casino pays off that way. It means that somewhere in the cavernous reaches of the casino there are a few machines with those odds. The rest are slots paying around 85 percent to 92 percent. And how do you find the machines with the 99 percent payouts? That's simple—pure luck. There's not really any other way, unless you belong to the Psychic Friends Network.

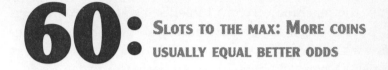

60: SLOTS TO THE MAX: MORE COINS USUALLY EQUAL BETTER ODDS

It's tempting to hoard coins as you play slots. And while this will ensure that you play longer, it won't guarantee you'll be a big winner. In fact, on certain types of slot machines, you should always play the maximum number of coins.

So-called pay-for-play slots come in two basic types: three-reel, three-pay lines and video slots with a variety of lines and symbols. The three-reeler gives you three chances to win because there's a payout on three lines rather than on one. But you're not likely to make much money if you only play one line instead of putting in enough coins to play all three. Besides, imagine how awful you'll feel if the big jackpot shows up on one of the reels you haven't paid for. Heck, they probably design the machines to tantalize you in that fashion. It's a way of saying, "I guess you'll put more coins in next time, right bucko?" The video slot has a variety of colorful symbols and characters—jungle animals, pirates, or something equally whimsical—but you won't necessarily win if you line up the symbols, unless you've put in the maximum number of coins. Again, spare yourself the agony of lining up something that does you no good because you didn't spring for it.

Even on traditional, one-reel slot machines, you should consider playing the maximum bet on each spin. The key is to study the machine's payout table. Some slots have a staggered payout ratio. If you bet more, you get proportionately more when you win. Always play the max coins on these machines. Other slots have a payout ratio that remains constant no matter how many coins you bet. If you get, for example, twenty coins for lining up three single bars with one coin in the machines, you'll get forty for two coins and sixty for three. You're still better off playing the maximum on these slots because the payouts will be bigger if you win. But if you're more interested in making the fun last, then you can stick with fewer coins on these machines. Just don't kick yourself if you hit a jackpot with one coin in the machine and realize that you're going to walk away a lot poorer than if you'd been less cheap in the first place.

If you're going to place the maximum bet on each spin, make sure you choose a machine with a denomination that fits your budget. You can go through $60 in four spins on a $5 slot machine with a three-coin maximum bet. If that sounds at all painful to you, then stick to quarter or nickel slots. On the other hand, you should also note that playing one coin in a high-denomination machine could win you more than three coins in a lower-denomination machine. However you choose to play, make sure you set a loss or win limit and stick to it.

61: PLAY PROGRESSIVES CONSERVATIVELY: THE LIFE AND TIMES OF PROGRESSIVE SLOTS

The story is always the same, which means it must be an urban myth. A man is waiting for his wife to finish her roll of quarters on a slot machine, and he decides to put his last three bucks into one of the casino's MegaBucks slots, which have payouts of $5 million or more. The jackpot's up past $18 million, and the buzz is that it will hit any day. The guy who's killing time doesn't know any of this. He doesn't care. He's just bored. He puts in his $3, lines up four MegaBucks symbols, wins nearly $20 million, and leaves with a cocktail waitress on the next flight to Tahiti. Okay, that last part isn't usually included in the myth.

MegaBucks is a progressive slot, one with a jackpot that grows, usually by the second. Progressives are typically linked together, and every coin that goes into one actually goes into the pot for all of the machines. Flat tops, or straight slots, offer a set jackpot that doesn't change. These are individual machines not hooked to others.

Independent machines will not have jackpots that allow you to retire, that's true. But MegaBucks and other progressives don't pay out as much for smaller jackpots because they hold onto their money for the monster payouts. Consequently, if you play a progressive, you're probably not going to win big, unless you WIN BIG. And your odds of doing that are about the same as your odds of being the first earthling to visit Uranus. If you're playing for fun, stick to flat tops. That guy who wins $20 million with three bucks doesn't exist. But if he does . . . could you spare three mil or so until next payday?

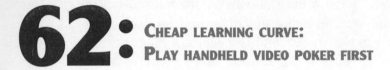

62: Cheap learning curve: Play handheld video poker first

Every convenience store, gift shop, and supermarket in or near Las Vegas can be guaranteed to have at least one item: cheap, handheld video poker machines. Invest in one that's most like the kind you'd like to play in a casino. For example, video slots can offer tens or better, jacks or better, deuces wild, or jokers wild. You can find handheld examples of each of these, probably for less than ten bucks apiece.

The advantage of handheld video poker is that it's about the only game you can play for free that's an exact mirror of its casino counterpart. Sure, you can find handheld blackjack, but most likely it won't give you a lot of options. You might be able to double down, but you probably won't be able to split pairs. For that matter, playing a machine and playing in the casino are far from the same. Handheld blackjack prowess won't make you a playa at the blackjack table. And while most casinos will have video blackjack, it's not a very popular game.

You can probably find handheld video poker at your local Wal-Mart. Pick one up before you get on the plane for Sin City. Play it constantly, preferably with the annoying beeping sounds off, until you figure out strategies that work for you. You can take chances—try to complete inside straights, for instance—without it costing you five quarters. Most likely you'll discover that inside straights are rarely filled, and you won't be as likely to go for them once you get to the casino. Any lesson that can help you win money—or at least not lose it—is a good lesson.

You'll also learn another lesson. Most handheld video poker starts you out at a certain number of points. Then it's up to you to build on them . . . or to lose them. What you'll find is that, over time, no matter how many points you amass, you'll ultimately wind up with zero. The moral of the story is quit while you're ahead. It won't cost you anything to keep playing handheld video poker until you've taken your windfall back to nada land. But imagine if those points were cold, hard cash.

For the most part, video poker—handheld or in the casino—is no substitute for the living, breathing version of the game played against other players. If you're a total babe in the woods, it can help you to familiarize yourself with the ranking of the hands and with strategies for attaining them. For table poker, you're best advised to get together with your buddies and play a close facsimile of the real game. Handheld video poker will prepare you for the money-spewing-out variety in the casino.

Finally, handheld video poker will give you a cheap lesson in just how addictive gambling can be. Once you pick up the little bugger, you'll find it impossible to put down. Minutes, heck, hours, will pass as you play. It's a great way to make your Vegas flight pass quickly. But it's not likely to work as an excuse when your wife asks why you still haven't mowed the lawn.

63: ODDS-ON VIDEO: CHOOSE THE BEST VIDEO POKER ODDS

Video poker machines are omnipresent as slots in most casinos. The machines all may look the same, but they're not. When you're looking for a machine on which you can hit big payouts, you're not looking for one that's hot. You're looking for a 9/6. If you stroll among the video poker terminals, look at the payout tables, which tend to be prominently displayed. If you insert one coin and get paid eight for a full house and five for a flush, then skip that machine. Seek instead one that pays nine for a full house and six for a flush, with a one coin bet. It's a no-brainer. One simply pays out more than the other for the same thing. Casinos count on newcomers not paying any attention to the difference. Don't be a simp.

The house edge on 9/6 machines is a low .5 percent. But to take full advantage of that edge, you need to play the maximum number of coins for each bet. If you don't and you hit a royal flush, the edge goes in favor of the house because you won't get the bonus that's typically paid out for a royal flush. For example, on a typical jacks or better 9/6, you'll get 4,000 coins if you hit a royal flush. By contrast, if the royal flush payout were based solely on multiplying by five the number of coins you'd get for a royal with one coin in, the payout would only be 1,000. If a machine doesn't pay off a bonus for royals with max coins bet, then choose another machine.

Some video poker machines are progressives, meaning they have a jackpot for a royal flush that gets progressively bigger. But you only win the progressive jackpot if you're playing with the maximum number of coins. You may play poker at the tables for weeks without seeing a royal flush, but they occur with some regularity on video poker machines—roughly one out of every 30,000 hands. That's a lot, yes. But remember, countless numbers of folks have played your machine throughout the day. You may be lucky number 30,000.

There's one final strategy for picking a machine with player-friendly odds. Choose one that's in the heart of the action. Just like slots, video poker machines can be set tight—meaning they don't pay out much—or loose—meaning they'll hit frequently. It's impossible by sight to tell which machines are loose, but you can usually pick entire rows of machines that are tight: They're the ones off the beaten path, say, near the bathrooms. Part of casino psychology is to put winners in the midst of the largest groups of people, so a loose machine in no-man's land would do little or nothing to entice others to try their luck.

64: Kick out the jams: Why you should never keep a "kicker"

Video poker is very similar to the real thing, but it's not exactly the same. For one thing, Video poker machines won't have an overpowering smell of cheap cologne emanating from them. The max bet on most machines is five coins, while you could lose huge sums of money on just one hand of poker against opponents. You don't have to worry about tight or loose players, just tight or loose computer chips—and unfortunately there's no way to bluff those.

And then there's the kicker, a high card you'd likely keep with a pair when playing poker at the tables. It's a good idea to hold a kicker when you're playing the real thing because poker all too often winds up being a boring battle of pitiful pairs. In the movies, it seems like every other hand is a royal flush or four of a kind. In real life, these don't come up all that often. So a kicker can often mean the difference between winning and losing because it breaks a tie.

There are no ties in video poker, but you may still feel an overpowering urge to keep your kickers. Don't do it. Ever. Never. When playing video poker, get rid of your kickers and give yourself the maximum chance to get three of a kind, a full house, or four of a kind to go with that pair that you most definitely should hold onto.

65: DON'T BE AFRAID TO DISCARD: THE ART OF MAKING THE BEST VIDEO POKER CHOICES

So many cards. So many choices. So many free drinks. What's a player to do? Well, relax. What follows is a handy dandy guide to the best strategy for jacks or better 9/6 flattops, the most common video poker machines in the average casino. First of all, be sure you understand how to keep and how to discard your chosen cards. On some video poker machines, you keep the cards by discarding the ones you don't like—often by touching the screen over those cards. But on some machines, you touch the cards you want to keep. If you get mixed up, screw up, and lose out on a royal, you will hate yourself in the morning. Actually, you'll hate yourself right away. Why wait until the morning?

If you're dealt four cards to a royal flush, discard the fifth in all cases, even if you have a standard flush. A flush pays a fraction of what you can get for a royal flush with five coins played. Take your chances. Be bold. Go for the royal, you wild-eyed gambler, you.

If you have three cards to a royal flush, keep a jacks or better pair or higher hand—three of a kind, a straight—rather than hoping for lightning to strike twice. But if the other cards do nothing for you, get rid of them, cross your fingers and toes, and hope for the best.

If you have two cards to a royal, keep high pairs, four to a flush, or four to a straight instead. You have a better chance of winning with these. If the rest of your cards are garbage, then get rid of them and hope you've acquired enough good karma to get a royal flush in return.

Never break up a straight or flush unless you're one card away from a royal flush. If you think it's a good idea, then stop playing because obviously you are too drunk to play video poker. On the other hand, if you have a pair of jacks or better, keep it instead of four cards to a flush or straight.

Don't break up four of a kind, a full house, three of a kind, or two pair. Just get rid of the card that doesn't help you. If you have jacks or better, keep it in all cases, except for when you have four cards to the straight, flush, or royal flush.

As for low pairs . . . you don't win with them, but they could be your ticket to three of a kind or—joy of joys—a full house or even four of a kind. Keep low pairs over four to a straight, but get rid of low pairs if you have four to a flush or three or four to the royal flush.

If you get five cards that just plain suck, then save four to a royal or straight flush, three to a royal flush, four flushes, four straights, three to a straight flush, two cards to the royal, two cards jacks or higher or one card jack and higher. If you don't even have enough to get any of these, then discard all five, say a little prayer, and get five new ones.

LOUNGE ACT

Don't Bet on It . . .
What You Didn't Know about
Las Vegas Landmarks and Events

This lounge act raises the curtain on some of the most interesting aspects of Las Vegas history, events, and landmarks. Let's face it . . . A city as unique as Las Vegas is going to accrue a unique patchwork of people and events over the course of a century.

First you'll watch Frank Sinatra and Howard Hughes duke it out over a policy change Hughes enacts in the casino sometimes called the House that Frank Built. Reports of what happened between these two titans vary, but one thing's for sure . . . The outcome left Frank turning his back forever on the casino he once—literally—owned a piece of.

Then you'll turn to the single worst day of Las Vegas's history, the day of the great MGM Grand fire, which killed more than eighty people and led to some significant changes in fire safety within resort properties everywhere. You'll also learn about one of the great stains on the history of Sin City. Las Vegas made its reputation on the backs of entertainers, including some of history's most talented performers—Sammy Davis, Jr., Nat King Cole, The Ink Spots. But for many years, black artists couldn't even walk through the casino to get to the stage. They were forced to come in through service entrances. No African Americans could gamble in most casinos, which is why Las Vegas was once called the Mississippi of the West.

You'll also sneak a peek at some of Sin City's specters. Yes, even a city that blows up its past is reputed to have some ghosts. They run the gamut from nineteenth century Mormons to victims of the MGM fire to the ghost of one of the city's founders—Bugsy Siegel. On a related note, you'll take a tour of the city's so-called Neon Graveyard, a place the company that owns it denies exists. But it does, and it's filled with the garishly beautiful signs of yesteryear, ones that adorned casino properties that have been history for decades.

66:
HOWARD HUGHES VERSUS FRANK SINATRA: WHY FRANK DROVE A GOLF CART THROUGH A WINDOW AT THE SANDS

Senator William Clark made Las Vegas a town. Bugsy Siegel made the Strip what it is today. But Frank Sinatra actually owned Las Vegas and the Strip . . . or at least that's what he thought until Howard Hughes came along.

The so-called Bashful Billionaire began his casino empire with the Desert Inn. And then, in July of 1967, he bought the Sands for $14.6 million. Not long before, Sinatra had sold his 9 percent share of the casino because the state revoked his gambling license, rendering it illegal for him to own a casino.

Sinatra, who also was part owner of the Cal-Neva in Lake Tahoe, lost his license because he invited good buddy—and well-known Mafia boss—Sam Giancana to visit the bucolic lodge and take a load off. For some reason, the Nevada state gambling commission didn't look kindly on Sinatra's hospitality to a man in the commission's so-called black book. This log contained the names of folks who were not ever, ever, ever, under any circumstances, to darken the door of any Nevada casino.

Even after Sinatra sold the Sands he continued to visit. After all, he and the other Rat Packers had made it THE hot spot in Las Vegas in the early 1960s. When Sinatra and the gang were in the house, action at the tables afterwards didn't slow down until daybreak.

But Sinatra must have gulped when he learned that Hughes had bought the Sands. It's a significant understatement to say that Sinatra did not smile warmly if a thought of the reclusive billionaire wafted through the transom of his mind. When Sinatra first began to court the great love of his life, Ava Gardner, Hughes tried to steal her away from Ol' Blue Eyes. But Gardner—at least this time—remained true to Sinatra. If anything angered Sinatra more than another man trying to court away Ava Gardner, then history doesn't record it. And Hughes didn't like to lose, especially to someone he thought of as an undersized, overstuffed pipsqueak.

These titanic egos finally came to a head just after Labor Day of 1967. Sinatra was playing an engagement at the Sands, thanks to his friendship with the casino's entertainment director Jack Entratter and not because of Hughes.

Accounts differ concerning what Sinatra did after he learned that Hughes had made a change in casino policy. For years, Sinatra didn't have to worry about his pockets running dry while playing at the Sands. If he ran out of money, he simply signed markers and drew additional money from the casino cage. One day, the Chairman of the Board walked up to sign his IOU, and he was denied. Mr. Hughes's orders, he was told.

Sinatra was not a man known for his equanimity and patience. Some accounts say he stormed out of the Sands, found a golf cart that was used to carry baggage around to hotel guest rooms, and proceeded to drive the cart through one of the casino's plate glass windows. Other accounts include the golf cart story but say it was a drunken prank that happened before Sinatra's credit was revoked.

Accounts agree that Sinatra stormed through the Sands like a bull after a flapping red cape once he learned his credit was cut off. He pushed over tables. He queued through an alphabet of epithets. Finally, he turned over the table at which casino manager Carl Cohen sat. The burly former truck driver knocked the man once known as Swoonatra to the floor. The singer lost two teeth and soon after crossed the street to Caesars Palace, which became his new performance hall and gambling parlor.

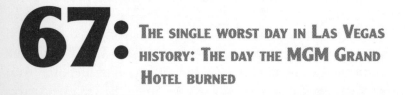

67: THE SINGLE WORST DAY IN LAS VEGAS HISTORY: THE DAY THE MGM GRAND HOTEL BURNED

The MGM Grand Hotel, across the street from the Flamingo Hilton where modern Las Vegas began, was 99 percent full on November 21, 1980. The seven-year-old hotel was among the most lavish on the Strip—twenty-six stories tall, 2,100 rooms, and filled with memorabilia from MGM's storied Hollywood past.

At 7 A.M., kitchen workers and wait staff thought they'd discovered a small, easily containable, grease fire. By 7:30 A.M., the fire began to spread throughout the hotel. A ball of flame headed toward the casino's main entrance. As slot machines melted, they released cyanide gas. On the main floor, fourteen people died in the flames and smoke. But most died on the upper floors, which the fire reached by climbing through the hotel's elevator shafts. The main killer that chilly November day was toxic fumes and smoke, not flames.

Ironically, many people in the MGM Grand first learned their lives were in danger as they rubbed sleep out of their eyes and watched a breaking news report on *Good Morning, America*. The hotel had Mac Davis in its main room that week, a biblical epic in its theater and even a jai alai court, but it didn't have smoke detectors, and most of its sprinklers were in the hotel's basement and shops area.

As smoke poured through the MGM's upper floors, some guests survived by placing wet towels in the cracks of their doors. Other guests made it to the roof of the building, and 235 were flown away in a helicopter. Iron workers constructing an addition to the MGM crossed scaffolding from the skeletal frame of a new hotel tower and helped more guests escape.

By 9:30 A.M., fire departments from Las Vegas, North Las Vegas, Henderson, Boulder City, Nellis Air Force Base, and from the rest of Clark County had the blaze under control. But those two hours marked the greatest death toll from a single event in Sin City's history—eighty-four died, and 700 were injured.

The MGM reopened less than a year later, in July of 1981. It was essentially the same as before, with one major difference: When it reopened, there wasn't a safer tall building in Las Vegas—or maybe the United States. Fire safety systems worth five million 1981 dollars had been installed. Other hotels built after the great fire also got equipped with high safety standards, and older ones were retrofitted.

By the early 1990s, the MGM Grand Hotel moved down the street and reopened as the world's largest hotel/casino. Its original location became Bally's Hotel and Casino. The jai alai court is gone, but Bally's still offers top-notch entertainment and theatrical events, as well as state-of-the-art fire safety.

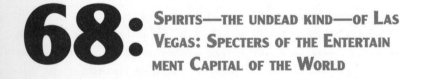

68: SPIRITS—THE UNDEAD KIND—OF LAS VEGAS: SPECTERS OF THE ENTERTAINMENT CAPITAL OF THE WORLD

No city celebrates life more than Las Vegas. Casinos aren't allowed to get old. They're just torn down at the sign of the first dust bunny. Youth is celebrated, with tans and plastic surgery making it last as long as possible. The absence of clocks and windows in casinos seem to make time stand still.

Crumbling old mansions are few and far between, as are moss-covered cemeteries filled with teetering tombstones topped with will o' the wisp. Besides, a procession of Jimmy Hoffa, JFK and a living, breathing Mickey Mouse could pass by most serious gamblers without so much as a pause on the handle of their slot machines.

But like any city with a storied—and Mafia-filled—past, it's not surprising that Las Vegas and its environs are said to host multitudinous spirits of the disembodied kind. For those interested enough in such things to take a break from trying to shave down the house advantage, Sin City offers some palaces of spooky pleasure.

Bally's is said to be haunted as a result of the 1980 fire that took eighty-four lives, back when the property was still the MGM Grand (see number 67). Most of the deaths were on upper floors of the main casino building, and some have reported screams, shadowy presences, knocking sounds, and the permeating odor of smoke there.

The oldest structure in Las Vegas is also thought to be haunted. The old Mormon Fort along North Las Vegas Boulevard, which dates from the mid-nineteenth century, is witness to whispered voices in the hours before daybreak. Maybe they're grumbling about how the nice mission they tried to start has become America's favorite den of iniquity.

The Flamingo Hilton is said to be haunted by the man who had it built, charming gangster Benjamin "Bugsy" Siegel (for more on Bugsy, see number 38). It was Siegel who had the vision of transforming a town of sawdust joints into a Mecca of sophisticated entertainment. It also was Siegel whose Fabulous Flamingo cost way more than he said it would and which closed temporarily because it leaked money like a sieve. Soon after it reopened and began doing brisk business, Siegel was dead from a hit by his former colleagues.

Even though Siegel was shot in Los Angeles, his ghost is said to roam the halls of the Flamingo Hilton, near the site of his no-longer-standing presidential suite. Bugsy walks the halls as a well-dressed, shadowy figure with his hands behind his back, his face bearing a mournful expression.

Nearby Boulder City also has a haunted hostelry, the Boulder Dam Hotel. It was built to house the families of those working on the Boulder Dam, which was later renamed for President Herbert Hoover. One of the hotel's founders, Raymond Spilsbury, drowned under mysterious circumstances in 1945. His death was ruled a suicide, but foul play was suspected.

When Las Vegas psychic Patsy Welding toured the Boulder Dam Hotel in 1980, she detected Spilsbury's spirit as one who sits at the window of a first-floor room, watching the goings-on of his hotel. Welding also reported sensing a young woman running in terror down a hallway and wearing only one shoe. When one of the rooms in the hotel was later remodeled, workmen discovered a hollow concrete block in the wall. Its contents: a single woman's shoe.

69: THE MISSISSIPPI OF THE WEST IS DESEGREGATED: THE MOULIN ROUGE ACCORD

There are two aspects of Las Vegas's history that vie for the greatest sin of Sin City: its Mafia-rich origins and a commitment to segregation that lasted until the 1960s. Even before Bugsy Siegel built the first classy joint on the Strip, Las Vegas was becoming the Entertainment Capital of the World. Performers with marquee recognition—regardless of race—were given more money for a short Vegas stint than they were likely to make with a longer engagement elsewhere.

But everything changed when the applause died down. "In Vegas, for twenty minutes, twice a night, our skin had no color," wrote Sammy Davis, Jr. in his autobiography, *Yes I Can*. "Then, the second we stepped off the stage, we were colored again." Davis and other black performers couldn't even walk through the casino to get to the stage. They had to come in and leave through the kitchen entrance. They weren't given luxury accommodations in the hotels they helped fill with eager gamblers. They had to find lodging with private homes in Las Vegas's predominantly African-American west side.

At least Davis, Nat King Cole, and others could be in a main room of a big-name casino. Other blacks were not welcome inside casinos, unless they worked inside them doing menial jobs. They gambled in clubs in west Las Vegas, like the Town Tavern, the El Rio, and the Louisiana Club. On May 24, 1955, the city's first integrated casino opened on Bonanza Road. The Moulin Rouge—topped by a large windmill—was wildly popular from the start. Blacks and whites alike gambled there in droves, and it had the best late-night nightlife in Sin City. While most casinos downtown and on the Strip offered two shows—one at 8 P.M. and one at midnight—the Moulin Rouge offered entertainment after 2 A.M. Headliners—Sinatra, Cole, Davis, and others—from the all-white casinos would play until dawn at the integrated gambling palace.

And then, six months later, the popular casino closed its doors. Explanations about its closing range from arguments among its owners to strong-arm tactics by the city's Mafia elite. But one thing is certain: The Moulin Rouge did not close due to lack of popularity. And its time as a history-making property wasn't over.

In 1960, Dr. James McMillan was the president of the Las Vegas chapter of the NAACP. He was the city's first African-American dentist, and he never shied away from a fight about principles. Inspired in part by the sit-in movement, begun on Feb. 1, 1960 in Greensboro, North Carolina, the Las Vegas NAACP announced that it would lead a protest on the Strip on March 26. City leaders freaked.

March 26, instead, became the day Las Vegas was desegregated. Concerned local and state leaders, along with casino operators and other business bigwigs, met at the Moulin

Rouge to discuss ending the city's policy of segregation. According to McMillan, the only reason the Mississippi of the West was desegregated was greed. Las Vegas's white leadership didn't want to do anything to derail the city's increasingly important convention business. Protests on the streets of Sin City might have made some corporations opt for Waukesha over Las Vegas.

A deliberately set fire nearly destroyed the Moulin Rouge in 2003. For years, different plans for the historic property's renovation were made and then went nowhere. Its former hotel rooms became apartments where drug arrests were made on a regular basis. After the fire, yet another group of investors spoke of resurrecting the Moulin Rouge, but once again, nothing happened. It seems unlikely this landmark in the history of civil rights will ever again be a thriving gaming and entertainment palace.

70: WHERE SILVER SLIPPERS GO TO DIE: YESCO's NEON SIGN GRAVEYARD

How many cities in America can boast not one, but two neon McDonald's signs? Only Vegas, baby! It's difficult to imagine Sin City without neon. It would be like Paris without the Eiffel Tower, Rome without the Coliseum, or Amsterdam without legal hookers. Parisian Georges Claude first used neon for commercial purposes, and commercial neon first appeared in the United States in 1923, at a Los Angeles Packard dealership.

But Las Vegas owes its title of the world's neon capital to a transplanted Englishman named Thomas Young, who founded the Young Electric Sign Company—called YESCO by almost everyone—in 1932, one year after gambling was legalized in the Silver State. A YESCO neon sign adorned Las Vegas's first legal gambling spot, the Boulder Club.

In 1951, YESCO's most famous sign rose above the Pioneer Club. Vegas Vic, a cowboy who points to the casino, still summons up Vegas for most folks. YESCO has also created the massive, twanging guitar that marks the Hard Rock Café Hotel and Casino, the Day-Glo mushroom cloud of the Stardust, and the disturbing skyscraper-sized clown that points to Circus Circus.

A city that stays as up-to-date as Las Vegas discards a lot of history. In a city where entire casinos are imploded, do you really think that neon signs will outstay their welcome? No way, Jose. Many of the signs no longer have properties to adorn. The Silver Slipper was gone soon after the lights of the slipper disturbed the sleep of Howard Hughes. The Hacienda's horse and rider was gone long before the casino itself was destroyed and replaced by Mandalay Bay.

In 1996, many of these classic signs began appearing at an outdoor museum along Fremont Street. The Neon Museum first put on display the Hacienda's horse and rider, a rather spectacular sign made up of neon and light bulbs. It was joined by Andy Anderson, mascot of Las Vegas's Anderson Dairy, and one of the lanterns from the old Aladdin, among others.

But what happens to the signs that don't find a home in the museum? They wind up in what's usually called the Neon Graveyard, one of Las Vegas's most famous unofficial landmarks. The graveyard is on YESCO's property (5119 Cameron Street), but if you call the company, they'll deny the landmark exists, even though it's clearly visible . . . and even though it's occasionally used as a backdrop for photo shoots. The company, understandably, wants to dissuade people from hanging around in its junkyard. Folks could get hurt. YESCO could get sued. So the Neon Graveyard isn't open to the general public, but more and more of the classic signs that speak of the golden era of Las Vegas are showing up downtown, in Glitter Gulch, where Sin City began.

PART 5:

SUCKER BETS AND GAMES WITH BALLS:
BINGO, KENO, WHEEL OF FORTUNE,
AND OTHERS

CASINOS ARE LIKE VAMPIRES WITH A BILLFOLD FETISH: They vant to suck your cash. The house edge means the casino will be triumphant over time. But there are some games at which you can almost guarantee that you, the fool, will soon part with your money.

These sucker bets include games that are attractive to newcomers because they require no skill. You can't just walk up to a blackjack table and expect to know how to play, for instance. But anyone can plunk down some cash on the wheel of fortune, or big six. Sometimes casinos offer promotions designed to separate you from the money you're supposed to use for unimportant stuff like mortgages and excessive credit card debt.

And then there are those games with balls: bingo and keno. These offer terrible odds, but they fall short of being mere sucker bets because of their "illustrious" history and opportunities to test theories of extrasensory perception and telekinesis. Can you use your mental powers to cause the right balls to get sucked out of their geese? Who knows? It's worth a try, anyway. Bingo has other metaphysical properties as well, such as sacred objects and lucky colors. And the game also has a social element. Between rounds, players discuss grandchildren and the ill-advised moves of American presidents. Games with balls aren't just games. For some folks, they're a way of life.

71:

You'd have better luck beating Pat Sajak at poker: The history and miserable odds of the wheel of fortune

Casinos borrowed the wheel of fortune from traveling fairs—the ones with crooked carnies shouting, "Hurry! Hurry! Step right up!" The game is perhaps the easiest to play in the casino, and it's usually near the entrance where folks can watch the wheel spin as they listen to the galvanic, ratcheting sound it makes. The wheel requires no skill, but you're best off avoiding it because it's a sucker bet. The best odds the game offers are terrible, and its worst are truly bleak.

The wheel of fortune is also called the big six because it contains fifty-four slots, each containing one of six symbols. The typical wheel has twenty-four $1 slots, fifteen $2 slots, seven $5 slots, four $10 slots, two $20 slots, and two jokers. Some casinos will have a slot marked "respin" in place of one of the jokers. If the wheel lands on this space, then all bets stay on the table, and the dealer spins again.

To play, simply place your chips down on one or more of the corresponding six symbols. Once all players have placed their bets, the dealer spins the wheel, and your fortune is in fate's hands. Round and round she goes. Where she stops, nobody knows. Winning requires nothing but luck, though the game offers a good opportunity to practice the art of mental telepathy or the power of desperate, self-serving prayer. When the wheel stops, the dealer takes the losing bets and pays off the winners.

If you've bet on the $1 symbol and it hits, then the payout is even money. The $2 symbol pays two to one, the $5 symbol five to one, the $10 symbol ten to one, the $20 symbol twenty to one, and the joker symbol forty to one or even forty-five to one at some casinos. Your best bet is the $1 symbol, which has the lowest house edge—though in this case "lowest" is relative. The house advantage for the $1 slot is 11 percent. The edge for the $2 symbol is around 17 percent, and the $5 symbol is more than 22 percent. The worst bet is on the $20 or the joker symbol. The house edge for these four spaces is 24 percent. By contrast, slot machines usually have a house edge of 15 percent or less.

All of that said, the wheel of fortune can be a pleasant diversion, if you limit your bets on it. It requires no skill but still gives you that sense of excitement, that chance for lady luck to smile upon you. The cheers from winning players and groans from losing players are entertaining as long as you're not one of the big losers. Of course, you can enjoy the response to the big six without being one of its groaning losers. Think of the wheel of fortune as the sorbet fine restaurants serve between courses to cleanse the palette. Or think of it as a long-running game show featuring Pat Sajak and Vanna White. Just don't think of it as an investment.

72: Keep your paycheck: Stay away from sucker bets like "double your paycheck"

Even though the days are gone when casinos practically gave away top-name entertainment to draw in suckers—er, gamblers—casino enticements still exist. Many of them are aimed at locals rather than visitors. For example, if you live in Las Vegas, you might get a voucher for free show tickets in the mail. Granted, it's not going to be for any of the Cirque du Soleil performances or shows of that ilk. But a free show is a free show, right?

The principle behind the vouchers is the same as the principle the city once had about low prices: Free or cheap shows are the cheese. Gamblers are the mice. The vouchers allow casinos to "double dip." First, you're tempted to gamble as you meander through the tables and machines on your way to the box office where you exchange the voucher for tickets. Then, you and your significant other are tempted to gamble on your way to the showroom, which of course is lodged behind scores of tables and slots.

A free Vegas show or lounge act is not a bad promotion, neither are "free money" promotions some casinos offer. A typical free-money offer will allow you to exchange a five-dollar bill for ten dollars. In some cases, you might get

$5 outright, without any cash outlay. What? Casinos giving away money? Well, not really. Casinos believe in this mathematical equation: Gambler with loose money + Hundreds of slot machines = Loose money (and more) goes into slot machines. When you get your free five spot, it's given to you in quarters. Now be honest. How many among us would have the fortitude to walk blithely past rows of slot machines with free money jangling in our pockets? You'd have an easier time whistling past the graveyard.

The most infamous enticement of all is the so-called "double your paycheck" promotion some casinos offer. You don't literally put your paycheck on the line. But you are playing with fire if you fall for this promotion. It's simple. If you cash your paycheck at the casino, you have the chance to double your money. Sometimes, a casino will use a special wheel of fortune for this promotion. One of the slots on the wheel will be marked something like "double your paycheck." If you hit it, you get twice your take-home pay. Other casinos use a scratch-off card, like the kind you get in other places for state Lotto. Or the casino might use a card with a pull-tab on it.

Whichever method a casino uses, the result is the same. If you take part in the promotion, your pockets get filled with loose cash . . . loose cash that actually isn't loose cash. It's your mortgage, your child-care expenses, your groceries for the week, your car payment, birthday gifts for your son or daughter. In short, it's money you can't afford to gamble with.

It's scared money—the kind that makes you pretty damn scared if you lose it.

And yet, there it is, weighing down your pockets. In a casino. And, gosh, what if you took that money, played a few hands of blackjack with it, and won enough to pay off six months of your mortgage? Well, that kind of thinking has dashed many a marriage and family. "Double your paycheck" is easily the most cynical bet in the casino. Avoid it at all costs.

73: Low down dirty dog: Red Dog Poker

As far as games requiring no skills go, Red Dog Poker isn't a bad choice. The house advantage is right around 3 percent, and you have the potential to win eleven times your bet—though the odds of doing that aren't great. Red Dog is also called In Between or Acey Deucy. Most folks are more familiar with the latter name, but casinos have probably taken to calling the game Red Dog Poker because it has the magic word "poker" in it. In fact, the game has nothing to do with poker, but your buddies back home don't have to know that. Just tell them you played a bunch of rounds of poker and were *muy macho* in the process.

To play Red Dog, find a table and make your initial bet. The dealer will deal two cards face-up. Let's say the cards are the same rank, two fours, for example. If the dealer's next card is another four, then you win and win big: eleven to one. If the third card is of a different rank, then you lose. Of course, it's not likely that three cards in a row of the same rank will be dealt. Most of the time, the two cards will be of different rank. If the first two cards are consecutively numbered, then it's a push. You get your bet back.

Let's say the two upturned cards are a three and a nine. You now can make an additional bet that the next upturned card will be of a rank between the two upturned cards. If the two face-up cards are a three and a five, then you shouldn't make the additional bet. But a three and a nine offer pretty good odds. If you bet $5 to begin with, then you can bet another $5 that the dealer will turn over a four, five, six, seven, or eight. At most casinos, your additional bet cannot exceed your original wager. If the next card falls between the other two, you win even money. If it isn't, you lose.

You shouldn't make the additional bet unless the spread is seven cards or more. Otherwise, you're likely to lose. If you decide to go for it, the payouts vary depending on the spread between the cards. For four or more, the payout is even money. A three-card spread pays two to one. A two-card spread pays four to one, and a one-card spread pays five to one.

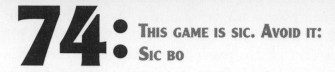

74: THIS GAME IS SIC. AVOID IT: SIC BO

Sic bo is Chinese for "lose money." Well, maybe not, but it ought to be. It's an easy game to play, but only one type of bet has a reasonable house edge—of 3 percent. After that, it's all uphill for you and smooth sailing for the casino. The game's name actually means "two dice," even though three dice are used to play it today. The dice are put into a shaker or small cage, tumbled about a bit, and poured out onto the table. The winning numbers are those facing up. At most sic bo tables, winning numbers are typed into a computer, which lights up the winning bets on the table. If you don't bet on the right numbers, darkness over your digits indicates you are a loser.

Sic bo has seven bets. The first is betting on a single number from one to six. If that number shows up on any one of the three dice, you win even money. If your number pops up on two dice, you win two to one. And if your number is atop all three dice, you get paid three to one. You can also bet on a combination of two numbers, called a two-face bet. This wager pays out at five to one. Or you can bet any pair. If you do, then the payout is typically eight to one. But "any pair" has a horse-choking house edge of 33 percent.

You can bet on a specific triple, which pays out at 150 to one. Or you can place a wager on any triple, which pays off at twenty-four to one. The house edge on both bets hovers around 30 percent. You can also place a bet on the three dice equaling a specific total between four and seventeen—totals of three and eighteen are losing numbers for this bet. The house edge on this "totals bet" ranges from an okay 10 percent to a cataclysmically awful 47 percent.

Finally, you can place a big bet or a small bet, predicting the total of the three dice will be between four and ten—for a small bet—or between eleven and seventeen—for a big bet. Once again, three and eighteen are losing numbers. These are the bets with the reasonable house edge of 3 percent, but the payout if you win is just even money. Take some time, learn to play blackjack, and head for those tables. Stay away from sic bo.

75: A LITTLE KENO WOULD BE KEEN-O: THE HISTORY OF KENO

Keno is one of the oldest games of chance, yet it was created for the same reason that states today offer lotteries and other forms of gambling: to make money for the government. Keno was invented by Cheung Leung to raise money for the army during the Han Dynasty of China some 2,000 years ago.

In its earliest form, keno was played with 120 Chinese characters, culled from the "Thousand Character Book." Think of it as a McGuffey's Reader or a Dick and Jane primer for kids in ancient China. Over time, the number of characters was reduced to ninety. When Chinese immigrants introduced the game to America in the nineteenth century, keno had eighty characters, the number a keno ticket bears today.

The game was popular, especially in San Francisco, despite the fact that it was illegal, because it gave players the chance to win a huge payout for a modest investment. The ancient characters became numbers once Americans discovered the game and started trekking into Chinatown to play. Americans were unfamiliar with the symbols, and they feared they were being cheated when they lost. The numbers one through eighty were substituted and remain to this day.

In its early days, players chose ten numbers from among the eighty on the card, and the payoff for catching all ten numbers was 3,000 for one. So a day's wages—$1—could earn you 3,000 bucks. Not bad for a day's work.

In the nineteenth century, keno numbers were printed on wooden balls, scrambled around by hand and put through a device called a goose. The goose, still used today, has a long, thin neck that sorts the balls. Since people mixed the balls by hand, there was concern about honesty. Casinos adapted the game slightly, exchanging numbered ping-pong balls for the wooden ones and forcing the balls through the goose by means of a stream of air that shimmies the ping-pong balls around like numbered popcorn.

After Nevada legalized gambling in 1931, keno was at first called Race Horse Keno. The Nevada Gambling Act expressly forbade lotteries, and keno is played much like a lottery, complete with numbered, air-popped ping-pong balls. Race Horse Keno was just semantics. Instead of players betting on numbers, the numbers were supposed to represent horses.

The horses ruse didn't last long because the federal government passed a law taxing off-track betting—which included Race Horse Keno. The game became simply keno, and the state of Nevada chose to ignore the game's similarity to lotteries.

Keno continues to be popular. In 1963, payout limits were $25,000. But since 1979, they've been $50,000. In some casinos, old showrooms have become keno parlors. Some visitors may lament the change, but you can bet that casino management will never rend its garments over substituting a big moneymaker for lounge singer launching pads.

76: Pick a number, any number: The basics of keno play

One of the first things you'll notice when you walk into most casinos are large overhead screens filled with the numbers one to eighty. Despite all of the action going on at floor level, the boards are hypnotic. Numbers pop up randomly on the screens, and then—once twenty numbers have appeared—the final number blinks. Then the screens go blank. The number at the bottom of the screens changes, and the process begins anew. The screens are keno boards. In some ways, keno is among the subtlest of casino games. While slots are—literally—awash in bells and whistles—keno is pretty quiet. But those boards are everywhere: the buffet, the restaurant, the bar—heck, sometimes even the john.

The screens are everywhere because winners must collect their money from one game before the next game begins, in most cases. That's how keno is different from a lottery. The play is much the same, but if you've got a winning lottery ticket, you've got plenty of time to collect your winnings. If you hit some numbers on a keno blank and you're not paying attention, then that's just too bad. Ya snooze, ya lose. But all you've got to do is devote a couple of gray cells to one of the omnipresent keno boards.

Keno is simple to play. It's one of the few casino games that actually comes to you. Keno runners circulate throughout the casino. They're usually—quite attractive—women bearing trays that don't hold food. Instead, the trays bear keno blanks—blank keno tickets. They'll also have dozens of black crayons. You can also find the blanks and crayons on every table in a casino's buffets, restaurants, and saloons.

In the upper-right-hand corner of the blank is a rectangle that says something like "Mark price here." Two large rectangles filled with squares are in the center of the ticket. The rectangles are divided by the words "Keno limit $50,000.00 to aggregate players each game." In other words, if two players win $50,000, each will get only $25,000. Sorry, that's gambling commission law. In the upper large rectangle, individual squares bear the numbers one through forty. The bottom rectangle includes the numbers forty-one through eighty. Why are the numbers divided like this? Who knows? It's one of life's great mysteries. At most casinos, the blanks will also offer at least one warning about collecting winnings immediately after a game.

One of the most popular keno tickets is called a five-spot because the player chooses five numbers. Of course, you don't have to play a five-spot. Depending on the casino, you can pick from a maximum of ten to twenty numbers. But if you want to play a five spot, here's what you do: In the upper-right-hand-corner rectangle, put in the amount you want to bet. At most casinos, the least a player can wager is 70 cents. But let's say you decide to bet $1. Write the number "1" in the blank. Don't add a dollar sign. In the two large rectangles, pick five numbers, any five numbers, and put an "X" through them with the black crayon. In the space to the right side of the large rectangles, write the number five, to indicate you've chosen five numbers.

Then hand the ticket to the keno runner or take it up to the keno writer in the keno lounge. Keep in mind that this original, or master, ticket is not valid for play. You've got to hand it to the runner or writer, and in exchange you'll receive a duplicate ticket that contains the date and the game number. Double check it to make sure everything on the duplicate ticket is correct. If a mistake has been made, it's your responsibility to catch it.

One you have your duplicate ticket in hand, just sit back and watch one of the keno screens. Then see if any of your five numbers come up. For a five spot, the typical jackpot for a $1 game is: Hit three and win back your buck. Hit four and get $14. Hit all five and win $720. Rate cards that show payoffs are as plentiful as keno blanks and crayons. If you win, immediately take your ticket to a runner or to the keno cage, turn in your ticket and collect your winnings. If you lose, simply curse, tear up the ticket and deposit the shredded paper into the nearest trash receptacle.

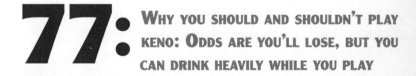

77: WHY YOU SHOULD AND SHOULDN'T PLAY KENO: ODDS ARE YOU'LL LOSE, BUT YOU CAN DRINK HEAVILY WHILE YOU PLAY

As Richard Nixon used to say, I want to make one thing purrfectly clear: Keno odds are lousy, with a capital "L." The house has a very high advantage whenever some sucker fills out a keno blank. No wonder those keno screens are in every nook and cranny of a casino. Odds vary, depending on how many numbers a casino lets you pick or any other restrictions some gambling halls place on the game. But, generally speaking, the house advantage is—at best—22 percent and—at worst—as much as 50 percent. Yikes.

The odds of hitting one number out of twenty are pretty good, around three to one. The odds of you hitting all the numbers on a five-spot are 1,550 to one. These odds aren't terrible, compared, say, to the likelihood of being visited by Ed McMahon bearing a large check from Publishers Clearing House. But even if you hit all five numbers, you won't be rich. You'll get between $700 and $800, a nice little windfall, but peanuts by casino standards. To win big money, you'll have to pick at least fifteen numbers and hit all fifteen. The odds of doing this are 400 million to one. Double yikes.

So why would anyone want to play keno? Why is it such a popular game? For many reasons, actually. For one thing, it's easy. Craps tables can be daunting even to regular gamblers, but a four-year-old could play keno. The game is also the only one in a casino that comes to you. Pick pretty much any spot within a gambling hall, and a keno runner will cross your path. The game is cheap. At most casinos, you can bet as little as 70 cents per game. For roughly the price of an evening showing of the newest blockbuster, you can play ten games of keno. After that blockbuster, you'll probably just feel disappointed at how lame the film was compared to its preview. After ten games of keno, you probably won't be rich, but at least you had the chance to make some money for nothing.

Keno also gives you the illusion of having some control over the outcome of a game of chance. After all, who picks the numbers on your blank? You do, of course. Even though, rationally and logically, you know that the odds of picking twenty numbers and then catching all twenty are slightly better than your odds of chasing a large white rabbit down a hole that leads to Wonderland, there's still a visceral thrill as you sit there considering what numbers to X through with your black crayon. Heck, maybe the crayon adds to the fun. It's a totem, a touchstone of your childhood. Maybe casinos will tap into that aspect of keno's appeal someday, and start to offer a rainbow of color options. Then you could mark numbers with your lucky color.

The two best reasons to play keno are that it requires almost no brainpower, and it's relaxing. You can plop down in the keno lounge and play for hours while swilling down free or cheap drinks. To play blackjack or poker, you've got to keep your mind sharp. Slot machines do not pull their own handles. Miss a call in bingo, and you're in trouble. But you can fill out one keno blank, indicate you want to play multiple games with the same numbers—chosen carefully by you—hand over your money, and then all of your work is done. All you have to do is collect your winnings, and it's unlikely that you'll ever become inebriated enough to miss it if you catch five out of five numbers on a five-spot. And you don't even have to worry about the rule concerning picking up your winnings immediately after a game. Most casinos these days offer an option for "play and stray keno." If you play a minimum number of games and use the same numbers each time, you can have up to a year to collect your winnings. Life is good.

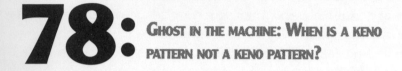

78: Ghost in the machine: When is a keno pattern not a keno pattern?

Keno is more than a simple game of chance with lousy odds. It's a portal to the paranormal or proof of the spiritual. If you decide to find a runner and mark up a few tickets, you'll notice that certain numbers pop up with some degree of regularity. As you sit there, drink in hand, you'll have a running interior dialogue that goes something like this:

Damn it . . . fifty-one again! Why didn't I bet on that lousy number . . . And seventy-six . . . I should have bet on that one anyway since it's the year I lost my virginity . . . Aw man, if twenty-two comes up again . . . What the heck? There it is again . . . Those numbers have come up three games in a row . . . How is that possible? . . . Maybe there really is a higher power in the universe . . . Lord God Almighty I'm born again . . . I promise to forego sin and attend church and tithe my earnings . . . which is why I need that runner back here again . . . I'll get a little more for the man upstairs . . .

There's no logical reason for why certain numbers or patterns of numbers come up frequently in the keno parlor. Each game is independent of every other game, which is why keno is a game of chance, not skill. The balls flail around in a wind machine until twenty of them are sucked out individually. A roulette wheel can become biased after months of continuous use. But frequently replaced ping pong balls? Circulating air? It must be a cosmic joke.

But you can laugh all the way to the bank. If you do see a pattern emerge, when certain numbers appear frequently, go ahead and pick them. But don't tempt fate by getting greedy. That's taking a supernatural gift and playing it for cheap. Stick to, say, a five-spot ticket. Go with the three or four numbers that keep showing up and then add another— your lucky number, for instance. If you've been living right, some of those numbers will come up again. Remember that for a five-spot ticket, the typical jackpot for a $1 game is: Hit three and win back your buck. Hit four and get $14. Hit all five and win $720. Go for that $720. It's not enough to retire on, but it's a sweet little windfall.

Get greedy, and you may tempt fate. It's not nice to fool with keno gods. Just as God is likelier to listen to earnest entreaties from families in need and nuns working to save the poor than to selfish requests for gambling windfalls, keno balls can smell greed. All too often, it seems like once you start betting big on emerging keno patterns, the numbers go off to keno heaven, never to appear again . . . while you're playing, anyway. So, maybe that's why you should play keno . . . to rekindle your belief in a higher power, something greater than yourself, something greater even than $3.99 unlimited buffets.

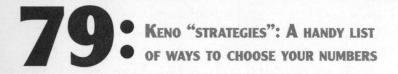

79: KENO "STRATEGIES": A HANDY LIST OF WAYS TO CHOOSE YOUR NUMBERS

There are only two "strategies" applicable to keno:

1. Don't play at all.
2. Choose your lucky numbers.

Since keno can be a fun, relaxing diversion as you drink multiple martinis, let's explore that second strategy. Most of us only have one, maybe two, lucky numbers. But if you want to play five or more numbers, what can you do? Relax. What follows is a handy list of lucky numbers. Pick and choose the ones that speak to you, then flag down a keno runner and get ready to win (or at least have lots of fun trying).

1. **Seven, four, one, seventy-seven, six:** July 4, 1776—Hey it's the birth of independence in the United States! What can be luckier for red-blooded Americans?
2. **Five, fifteen, sixteen, nineteen:** May 15 and 16, 1905—If you're playing in Las Vegas, then no numbers could be luckier. These are the dates of the land

auction that marks the birth of America's favorite adult playground.

3. **Twelve, one, two, nineteen, fifteen:** December 12, 1915—This is the date on which the Chairman of the Board first screamed at the people around him. Frank Sinatra was born on this date in Hoboken, N.J.

4. **Two, twenty-eight, nineteen, six:** February 28, 1906—For those who like the idea of Vegas's mob-filled past, pick these numbers. They correspond to the birth date of Benjamin "Bugsy" Siegel, the man who helped make a sleepy cowtown with gambling into Vegas, baby!

5. **Eleven, twenty-seven, nineteen, sixty-six:** November 27, 1966—The businessmen and businesswomen among you may instead prefer to celebrate the arrival in Las Vegas of Howard Hughes. He made Las Vegas respectable. But he also helped to lay the groundwork for Celine Dion to charge three-figure sums for shows in her very own theater.

6. **One, twelve, forty-one, nine, fifty:** November 24, 1950—The musical *Guys and Dolls* had its Broadway debut on this date. It features the song, "Luck Be a Lady." In the movie version of the musical, the song was sung—with some unintentional hilarity—by the late, great Marlon Brando.

7. **Three, one, nine, thirty-one:** March 19, 1931—You wouldn't even need these "strategies" if it weren't for

this date. It's the day that the state of Nevada legalized gambling within its borders.

8. **Seven, three, one, six, nine:** July 31, 1969—Elvis Presley didn't do so well in Vegas during his first visit in 1956. But he returned with a vengeance. On July 31, 1969, he debuted at the International (later the Las Vegas Hilton). He was a hit, a smash, he knocked 'em dead. Elvis became THE top draw in the Entertainment Capital of the World for several years.

9. **Eight, twenty, nineteen, six, four:** August 20, 1964—In a scene deleted from Quentin Tarantino's 1994 film *Pulp Fiction*, we learn that there are two kinds of people in the world: Elvis people and Beatles people. Just in case that's true, you could choose these numbers, since they correspond to the day The Beatles played Las Vegas for the first and only time.

10. **One, twelve, twenty-eight, nine:** November 22, 1989—During the 1980s, Las Vegas was in a sort of holding pattern. It still drew plenty of visitors, but it no longer seemed relevant. It was a sort of living history museum with slot machines. One date that vies for the birth of modern (post-modern?) Sin City is 11/22/89, the day Steve Wynn's Mirage opened, with 3,039 rooms. The Mirage created a new level of opulence in Las Vegas. It was a direct descendant of The Flamingo and Caesars Palace.

80:

And what was his name-o?
The history of bingo

Bingo is the one game of chance that everyone can accept, from church-going folks to inveterate gamblers. It's unlikely, for example, that you'll find a church financing its new wing with a craps tournament. But bingo? Sure, why not? Maybe it's this church association that makes bingo seem like the PG game in your typical R-rated casino.

But if you've ever watched a group of mature men and women playing a knockdown, drag-out game of bingo, then you know the game is not for sissies. Some sweet, little old ladies who say their prayers, tithe to their house of worship, and bake cookies for the sick will play fifteen bingo cards at a time and swear like drunken sailors on shore leave if someone else yells, "Bingo!" first.

It's believed that bingo has its roots in sixteenth century Europe as a type of lottery. Around the turn of the twentieth century, the game arrived in America and became a staple at traveling carnivals, where it was called "beano" because you marked your cards with dried beans. The winner would call out, "Beano!" The game changed its name thanks to a toy salesman named Edwin Lowe, who observed the game during the 1930s. He marveled at its simplicity and popularity.

During one round of play, an excited and flustered player shouted out, "Bingo!" instead of "beano." Lowe took the game and its new name and marketed it. By the 1950s, communities across the United States legalized bingo, and it turned into a popular fund-raiser. Bingo became a staple of church socials and community centers, spreading finally into casinos, where it's the most popular game with balls—beating out keno for that privilege. Bingo also became a staple of Indian reservations, before the days when tribes could feature all-out gambling.

There are even communities that sponsor cow pie bingo. For this version, a large grid on a field, resembling a bingo card, is constructed. Cows walk about, doing their thing—chewing a cud here, chomping on some grass there. Eventually, nature takes its course, and whoever's bought the spot where the first cow pie lands wins. Maybe they should just call that game craps instead.

81: C'MON, I 22, I 22, THAT'S ALL I...BINGO! AW CRAP: THE BASICS OF BINGO PLAY

Bingo's low-key thrills make the game popular with older folks. But it's a fun diversion for anyone. You can hear a pin drop as the game begins. As more numbers get called, a palpable buzz of energy permeates the room. Tension builds and builds until someone shouts the magic word and tension is released. Yes, it's kind of like sex. Maybe that's what makes it so popular. It's like a massive orgy performed among total strangers—many of them well past retirement age. Pretty kinky, huh?

Bingo is reasonably straightforward and simple. To play, you purchase a bingo card or cards. For some reason, four cards seem to be the norm. Each card has on it twenty-five squares, with the one in the middle marked "free" or "bingo." It counts automatically as a number for all players. At the top of the card is the word "bingo." The squares under the "b" range from one to fifteen; under "i" from sixteen to thirty; under "n" from thirty-one to forty-five; under "g" from forty-six to sixty; and under "o" from sixty-one to seventy-five. No number on an individual card is repeated, but several cards share similar numbers.

In most casinos, ping-pong balls marked one through seventy-five are circulated within a large plastic ball by a device called a blower. Balls come out of the cage one at a time, and a casino employee named a caller does her thing, calling out the numbers as they emerge from the blower. As the balls come out, they're placed on a masterboard, or rack, and generally, they're flashed up on an electric board. When one of the numbers on your card or cards is called, mark it with markers or rubber stamps, whichever the casino provides.

The traditional way to win is to fill five squares in a row, either horizontally, vertically, or diagonally. But casinos typically offer a wide array of bingo variations. There's four-corner bingo, wherein the first player to mark the four corner spots on her card is the winner. There's picture frame, where the object is to fill the outside numbers on the card, "framing" the ones in the center. And there's smiley face, where the object is to create a pattern that looks like . . . you guessed it . . . a smiley face. Make sure you know what pattern you're going for before you sit down to play. God help you if you call bingo and don't have it. If looks could kill, you'd be riddled with holes. Many casinos also offer a form of bingo called coverall or blanket bingo. The object of this one is to cover every spot on your card. The first to do so wins a progressive jackpot that can run into the thousands of dollars.

Bingo's odds are not the greatest. The house edge is 20 percent or more. But it's still a fun game nonetheless. Between games, you may actually get chatty with other players. After all, you've been through so much together! So, if you're playing bingo with visions of jackpots dancing in your head, then fuhgeddaboudit. But if you enjoy that growing feeling of tension followed by explosive release—and you want to experience this in a PG setting—then bingo is the game for you.

 **82: THE WORST SPOT IN THE HOUSE: PLAY BINGO WHERE OTHERS FEAR TO TREAD**

Bingo isn't at all about skill or ability. It's about luck, pure and simple. But there are a few ways you can ensure lady luck doesn't completely snub you. As long as cards aren't too expensive, play with more than one. It's true that your odds of winning are made only slightly better. But in a casino, anything (legal) that can turn odds in your favor is a good thing. You can also purchase some instant karma by understanding the payouts. If you take a game that costs $1 a card and pays $50 with 100 cards in play and contrast that with a game costing $1 paying $100 with 200 cards in play, you can see that your odds of winning are better in the first game. But the variance in payouts makes these games about even.

The single best way to increase your odds of winning at bingo is to have fewer opponents, so your mission—should you choose to accept it—is to play bingo at the remote or less popular places where others fear to tread. Is it uncomfortably hot in one casino's bingo parlor? Great! That can work to your advantage. Buy one of those hand-held fans, a few bingo cards, and you'll be too cool to fool. Is the temperature so cold that you could hang meat in the bingo parlor of another casino? Well, then, let the prospect of winning keep you warm and comfy. What's that? The bingo parlor at the You Bet Your Ass Hotel and Casino seems to be an afterthought, stuck into a remote corner of the building near the kitchen's exit to the dumpsters? Fan-frikkin-tastic! Enjoy yourself! When you're yelling Bingo! those dumpsters will smell like bouquets of roses. Uh oh. No free drinks being served? Hmm, we'll have to think about this one . . . Oh, what the hell. Play anyway. If you win big, you can buy yourself a distillery!

On the Las Vegas Strip, seek out older properties close to Sahara Avenue. Just past that giant martini-glass statue called the Stratosphere is what locals call "Naked City." It's like the Strip's id, a haven for the hallmarks of urban blight: pawn shops, strip clubs, by-the-hour motels. This no-man's-land between the Strip and Fremont Street doesn't have many casinos, but if you find one with a bingo parlor, then by all means, purchase a few cards and get down to business. If you get tired, you can always rest for a short while at a by-the-hour motel.

Another good place to play bingo if you love the game and want to win is the part of Fremont Street that's not within the Fremont Street Experience. Walk toward the dilapidated buildings and $18-a-night motels bearing signs warning guests not to entertain prostitutes in their rooms. The casinos you'll find on this spot of Fremont are not pleasure palaces with volcanoes and dancing water. But you came here to win some money, right? Leave the spurting fountains to the kids and tour groups. These properties are a low-roller paradise, featuring everything from $1-minimum blackjack to penny slots to cavernous and half-filled bingo parlors. These casinos may look dangerous, but for the most part, you should be safe. There are security guards around, and most of your fellow gamblers are locals who already know that the places to win are these holes-in-the-wall where the booze is cheap and the slots are even cheaper. Always be cautious and you will be fine.

83: It's in the cards: Find deals on multiple cards

Your chances of winning a round of bingo increase if you have more than one card, but not so dramatically that it makes sense to put your entire bingo bankroll on one game and as many cards as you care to afford. If you play in one of the nicer bingo parlors, you can expect to compete against 199 other cards, all inspected closely by opponents vying for the chance to scream the magic word. If you have one card, your odds of winning are a mere one in 200. If you have five cards, though, your odds increase to one in forty.

In truth, you're not really increasing your chances of winning so much as you're decreasing the likelihood of losing. You're paying five times as much to decrease your odds of losing from 199 out of 200 to a measly 195 out of 200. There's still a good chance you'll lose your money, and you're losing it five times faster with each round of bingo.

Before you play, do some research. Some casinos offer special rates on multiple cards. Even with those rates, you're just as likely to lose as you would be if you paid the same price for each card. But you ARE increasing your chances of winning, while spending less money for the privilege.

This is good. Somebody's got to yell bingo. It might as well be you.

You should be exceptionally vigilant for special rates on coverall bingo. This variety of the game requires you to fill every spot on your card—except the free space of course—in order to win. Often there's a significant jackpot should you win a coverall game. If the caller picks out fifty balls, then your odds of winning at coverall with one card are one in 212,086. Yikes. Even numerous cards won't guarantee that anyone wins a game of coverall, but the more you have, the luckier you can become. And if you're going to play anyway, then that's the way to do it: a good rate on multiple cards, either for a standard game or for the chance to win the big, big money at coverall.

84: BE MY LITTLE GOOD LUCK CHARM: FUN BINGO FETISHES

The best thing about all games of chance—especially games with balls—is that they give players a chance to test their powers of extrasensory perception and telekinesis. Folks who by the light of day don't have a superstitious bone in their bodies—they look with disdain on horoscopes and chuckle at cookie fortunes—will come on like the seventh son of a seventh son when they walk into a bingo parlor.

These sometimes bizarre, voodoo-like rituals make bingo fun, even if you think the game is way too tame and far too lame for your sophisticated self. Just enter the bingo parlor and pretend you're a cultural anthropologist, studying the mysterious rituals surrounding games played by a long-lost blue-haired tribe. Craps may have the action. Blackjack may have the best advantage for serious gamblers. But no game is more colorful than bingo.

Some players swear by lucky numbers. Other players believe calls will go in their favor depending on the time of day, day of the week, outside weather conditions, and/or indoor temperature. Other players believe they gain an advantage due to certain power colors. For example, one woman may prefer wearing scarlet from head to toe, while another is quite certain that a lemon-yellow blouse and purple hat give her the edge. Players also swear by a lucky article of clothing. If they leave their house or hotel room without their chartreuse scarf, then it's no way, no play. It's akin to a baseball player believing he's become an RBI powerhouse because of his lucky socks, which he wears until they stand up by themselves. The difference is, those socks may very well give the baseball player the psychological edge that allows him to slam line drives. But penny loafers with the left showing heads and the right showing tails will not sway the balls as they flutter around in the blower.

The most interesting thing for the armchair anthropologist to observe is good luck charms, an odd mix of voodoo, consumerism, and Christianity. One woman, for instance, will have her lucky color and secret away a miniature plastic horseshoe in her pocket. Before each number is called, she'll look up to heaven and entreat the Lord to help her win. For extra help, she may rub the horseshoe for luck. Some players use photos of their children or grandchildren as their good luck charms, which is one of the hallmarks that make bingo such a communal game. After someone calls bingo and the groaning stops, folks will talk about their charms or their photos. They'll laugh at their own superstitions. But just wait until the next game is called, and those amulets again become guarantees that God and good fortune will smile down upon them this day.

LOUNGE ACT

GAMBLING IS EVERYWHERE . . .
WHAT YOU DIDN'T KNOW ABOUT
THE SPREAD OF GAMBLING

For nearly fifty years, table gaming and slot play in the United States were synonymous with the Silver State, especially its unofficial capital, Las Vegas. These were halcyon days for Sin City, when it had no competition. It still tried hard, mind you, aiming to be the glitziest and most glamour-filled destination in a country also boasting New York City, New Orleans, San Francisco, Chicago, and Los Angeles—not an easy task.

But starting in 1978, when Atlantic City, New Jersey, opened its first legal casino, gambling began to spread across the country—some would say like a welcome wildfire, others would say like a pestilent plague. Gaming spread to riverboats and Indian reservations, to remote counties in remote states, eager to grab and devour a piece of the gambling pie.

And whether you believe gambling trumps money as the root of all evil or think it's the coolest, hippest thing a person who doesn't want to visit Nevada's legal brothels can do, it hardly matters. Gambling is everywhere—except in Utah and Hawaii. And chances are, the power of gambling will ultimately be stronger even than Joseph Smith or the goddess Pele.

85: HOT-LANTIC CITY:
ATLANTIC CITY BECOMES VEGAS EAST

Around the turn of the twentieth century, Atlantic City was one of the East Coast's favorite vacation spots. The seaside town's boardwalk was so famous that the street names along it were borrowed for the board game Monopoly. Some of Frank Sinatra's earliest professional performances were on Atlantic City's Steel Pier.

By the 1950s, Atlantic City was going to seed. Erstwhile pleasure palaces were crumbling like ancient ruins. Between 1960 and 1970, the city's population declined by 20 percent, and available hotel rooms declined by 40 percent. Between 1965 and 1975, Atlantic City lost 4,500 jobs. Housing values dropped steeply, and older areas of the city were in near-total decay.

With Atlantic City's days seemingly numbered, legalized gambling became the favorite panacea of the town's movers and shakers. It will attract new tourists who will spend tons of money, they said. In 1974, the state legislature passed a referendum proposal to legalize gambling throughout New Jersey, but it failed. Opposition forces that said that gambling would bring corruption with it convinced voters. It was easy to believe in the year that Richard Nixon resigned from the presidency.

In 1975, state assemblymen Charles Worthington and Steven Perskie—both from Atlantic City's Atlantic County—sponsored a bill for a new referendum. This time, the legislature attempted to counter voters' fears by focusing on the economic boosts and new jobs that gambling could bring. In 1976, Perskie coauthored another bill to make gambling legal only in Atlantic City. The bills were merged. Pro-casino forces—including international casino operators as well as city movers and shakers—spent millions on a publicity campaign designed to make legal gambling in Atlantic City look as warm and fuzzy as possible.

The new referendum passed. The state officially legalized Atlantic City gambling on June 2, 1977. Funds from gaming would be used for state and local social programs. The first casinos in "Las Vegas East" opened in 1978. And while gaming did bring tourists back to the boardwalk and create new jobs, it didn't create a renaissance in Atlantic City's deteriorating sections. Land speculation destroyed many low-cost housing options. Skyrocketing rents drove out many mom-and-pop businesses.

Today, glitz and glamour front the boardwalk. The Trump Taj Mahal is lord over all it surveys, or it will be, as long as Trump remains solvent. World-class performers once again sing near the Steel Pier. Tourists are carted from casino to casino by rickshaws—a holdover from Atlantic City's glory days. But take a few steps down one of the city's Monopoly streets, and you'll still see plenty of urban blight:

trash-strewn streets, empty and crumbling storefronts, liquor stores guarded by more iron bars than Alcatraz. For Atlantic City, legalized gambling has been a mixed blessing.

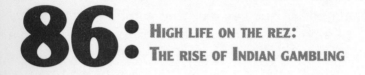

86: HIGH LIFE ON THE REZ: THE RISE OF INDIAN GAMBLING

Long before Europeans came to what is now the United States, Indian tribes across the land integrated games of chance into tribal ceremonies or—like folks today—just played them for fun. As America grew, Indians were pushed onto reservations and stripped of their culture and means of making a living. But in recent years, gambling has become a dominant industry on reservations, helping to fund cultural restoration projects as well as to pump a much-needed source of revenue into impoverished communities.

Modern tribal gaming traces its roots to bingo parlors in the early 1980s. As more and more states adopted lotteries to raise money for statewide social and educational programs, tribes in California and Florida borrowed that concept for themselves. They opened bingo parlors, offering payouts greater than those allowed by the states. When the states tried to shut down the bingo operations, the tribes sued in federal court: *Seminole Tribe vs. Butterworth* (1979) and *California vs. Cabazan Band of Mission Indians* (1987).

The court's ruling on both cases effectively gave tribes the right to operate games of chance on reservations, free of state control—as long as the games offered on reservations were not criminally prohibited within the state. In 1988, Congress passed the Indian Gaming Regulatory Act, which both recognized tribes' rights to operate gaming industries AND limited those rights. The act recognizes tribes' sole ownership of casinos on reservation land, but it requires the tribes to negotiate with their states the regulation of those casinos. As Indian gaming has become increasingly profitable, states have put more and more pressure on tribes to share some of the wealth.

While many tribes across the country have found new sources of wealth and cultural reconstruction through glitzy casinos, no tribe has been more successful than the Pequots of Connecticut. Although the tribe only became federally recognized in 1984, the Pequots were noted in the journals of early explorers, which described them as numerous, warlike, fierce, and brave. The tribe's name translates to "destroyers." In 1637, English colonists in the area waged a full-scale war on the tribe, which had been responsible for raids that killed several people. Nearly 1,000 members of the tribe—including women and children—were killed by militias from several colonies. In 1638, the Treaty of Hartford forced the remaining Pequots to become members of other, peaceful tribes. They were forbidden to refer to themselves as "Pequots." The tribe's land became part of Connecticut.

But the tribe persisted, finally gaining federal recognition in the mid-1980s. In 1986, the tribe opened a bingo hall with a $4 million loan from the Arab American Bank. Just two years later, the Pequots repaid the loan, and the bingo parlor was raking in $14 million. After the federal government passed the Indian Gaming Regulatory Act, the Pequots began to negotiate with the state of Connecticut to open a full-fledged casino.

A 1992 pact allowed the tribe to establish a casino on its 4,000 acres of land in southeastern Connecticut. The state, in return, could place law enforcement on the casino property. Foxwoods High Stakes Bingo and Casino opened in 1994. By the turn of the twenty-first century, it employed 10,500 people and 20 million people were visiting each year. Its revenues topped a billion—with a "b"—dollars annually. Not bad revenge for a tribe numbering 300 members, whom colonists thought they had destroyed more than 400 years ago.

87: LOSING MONEY ON THE MISSISSIPPI: HOW THE MAGNOLIA STATE BECAME A GAMBLER'S PARADISE

The Rev. Jesse Jackson once called Tunica County, Mississippi "America's Ethiopia." It was the poorest county in the country's poorest state. Nearly 70 percent of adults didn't have a high school diploma, and roughly one-quarter of the homes in the county lacked indoor plumbing. Situated not far from Memphis, Tennessee—called by Southerners the "capital of north Mississippi"—Tunica County is located on the banks of the mighty Mississippi. It's the northern tip of the delta, located on the famous Highway 61, home to blues legends galore. One of Bob Dylan's best albums, *Highway 61 Revisited*, pays homage to what was and what remained a sleepy highway until 1992.

In 1990, Mississippi authorized casinos along the Mississippi River and the Gulf of Mexico. Two years later, the first gambling palaces arrived. Soybean and cotton crops now bask in the glow of bright lights from massive casinos and their marquees, which bear the name of some of the world's foremost entertainers. At least 1.2 million people travel up and down that no-longer-sleepy highway of legend. As the twentieth century ended, Tunica County boasted thirty riverboat casinos. Of course, they're not really riverboats. They're large buildings connected by walkways from the bank. Actually, they're neither boats nor buildings. They're cash cows, raking in more than $2 billion annually.

Mississippi has gone out of its way to promote casino gambling. While most states try to control the spread of gambling, the Magnolia State has let free enterprise dictate how many casinos tie up at the dock, and how well each performs. In addition, Mississippi only collects 8 percent of its casinos' revenue, one of the lowest rates in the country. And the state charges casinos a mere $5,000 every two years to renew their licenses.

Louisiana, by contrast, collects around 20 percent of its casinos' revenue, and license renewal is $100,000 annually.

But some critics say the state's windfall has only benefited its white citizens. Unemployment within the county is nearly 15 percent, the same as when the first casinos opened. The riverboat casinos traditionally have hired from outside the majority-black Tunica County. The county seat of Tunica boasts thirty millionaires and almost no poor whites, and the town is 74 percent white. Blacks have a lock on poverty, especially in the county at large, which is the reverse of Tunica itself: 74 percent black to 26 percent white.

88: Gambling is everywhere: What you can wager on in these United States

Efforts to increase or shut down the spread of gambling across the country are endless. So by the time you read this, the number of gambling choices in individual states could be different. But as Bob Dylan once famously said: The times they are a-changin'. It's a safe bet that more—not less—gambling will be allowed ultimately in our friendly fifty states. Lotteries aren't included in this list, just gambling that requires going into businesses other than convenience stores.

Alabama has casinos—featuring bingo and electronic gaming—on Indian reservations. The state also offers dog tracks.

Alaska has pull-tab gaming and bingo parlors on several Indian reservations.

Arizona has run-the-gamut gaming at more than twenty Indian reservations. The state also has dog tracks and horse tracks.

Arkansas has a dog track and a horse track.

California has around 130 casinos on Indian reservations. The state also has cruise-ship gambling and several horse tracks.

Colorado has nearly fifty casinos centered in Black Hawk, Central City, and Cripple Creek. They offer all types of gaming. The state also has several dog tracks and one horse track.

Connecticut is home to two of the "250-pound gorillas" of Native American gaming: Foxwoods and Mohegan Sun. The state also has two dog tracks.

Delaware has three horse tracks at which electronic gambling is allowed.

Florida offers a variety of gambling choices: six Indian casinos, gambling cruises, real cruises that also offer gaming, dog tracks, dog tracks called "racinos" that offer additional gaming, horse tracks, horse track "racinos," and even Jai-Alai.

Georgia offers two casino cruises.

Idaho offers electronic gaming and bingo at fewer than ten Indian casinos. The state also has several horse tracks.

Illinois has several riverboat casinos and a number of horse tracks.

Indiana has several riverboat casinos and two horse tracks.

Iowa has several full-service casinos, both on reservations and in stationary riverboats. The state also has two dog tracks and one horse track.

Kansas has five Indian casinos, one dog track, and three horse tracks.

Kentucky is one of America's horseracing capitals, featuring a number of tracks. Louisville is home to the famous Churchill Downs, site of the annual Kentucky Derby.

Louisiana is where widespread gambling first took root in the United States. It's been legalized, criminalized, and legalized again. At this point, it's legal on stationary riverboats and Native American casinos. The Big Easy has four riverboat casinos. The state also has two horseracing tracks and two horse track racinos, which also offer slots.

Maine has one Native American casino featuring bingo and pull-tab gaming. Vacationland also has cruise-ship gambling and two horse tracks. The state approved racinos in the spring of 2004.

Maryland has five horse tracks.

Massachusetts has gambling cruises leaving from Gloucester and Lynn. The state also has two dog tracks and three horse tracks.

Michigan has several Indian casinos. The Motor City itself boasts three casinos. The state also has several horse tracks.

Minnesota has just over twenty Native American casinos and one horse track racino, which features a variety of table games.

Mississippi is one of the stationary-riverboat-gambling capitals of the world, boasting more than thirty "floating" palaces.

Missouri has an even dozen riverboat casinos.

Montana has around 150 Native American casinos featuring electronic gaming. The state also has five horse tracks.

Nebraska has three casinos and five horse tracks.

Nevada. Enough said.

New Hampshire has three dog tracks and two horse tracks.

New Jersey is home to a little ol' town called Atlantic City. The state also has four horse tracks.

New Mexico has a number of Indian casinos and four horse track racinos.

New York has several Indian casinos, as well as casino cruises, gaming on cruise ships, horse tracks, and horse track racinos.

North Carolina has one bingo parlor and one casino, both in Cherokee.

North Dakota has around thirty casinos, and Fargo boasts one horse track.

Ohio has seven horse tracks.

Oklahoma has about forty Native American casinos and four horse tracks.

Oregon has about ten Indian casinos, one dog track, and a half-dozen horse tracks.

Pennsylvania has five horse tracks.

Rhode Island features one casino in Newport and a dog track racino in Lincoln.

South Carolina has one Indian bingo parlor/pull-tab-gambling casino in Rock Hill and two casino cruises that leave from Little River.

South Dakota has around fifty casinos and two horse tracks.

Texas features an Indian casino, casino cruises, dog tracks, and horse tracks.

Virginia is home to the Colonial Downs horse track in New Kent.

Washington has a number of casinos, gaming on cruise ships, and five horse tracks.

West Virginia has two dog track racinos and two horse track racinos.

Wisconsin has more than twenty-five Native American casinos and two dog tracks.

Wyoming has one Indian bingo parlor and one horse track.

89:
WE DON'T NEED NO STINKING GAMBLING: TWO STATES WITH NO CHANCE TO TRY YOUR LUCK OUTSIDE OF A SINGLES BAR

You want to go on a gambling vacation, but Sin City's not your bag, baby. So you're thinking: Who needs those stupid lounge acts and stuff-yer-face buffets? The Midnight Idol? Never heard of him. Why the hell is there a big city in the middle of the desert anyway? What if they run out of water while you're trying to get those stakes up higher? They may *say* it's a dry heat out there, but no matter what anybody says, 115 degrees is too hot for human beings. Only lizards and horny toads should be living in that god-forsaken place.

How about Mississippi? Hmm. Isn't that the South? I've heard all kinds of stories about the South. Besides, they've only got riverboat gambling, and what if the boat capsizes or something? I don't want my last act on earth to be pulling the handle on a slot machine and losing three bucks.

Atlantic City? That could work. The casinos are planted firmly in the ground. I like that. But I've heard Atlantic City's not exactly what folks are talking about when they refer to

New Jersey as the Garden State. What if I get mugged or something, after I've won a fortune and before I can give it to St. Anthony's Orphanage, which of course is what I'd do with my ill-gotten gains?

I've got it! Hawaii! I can lay around on the white-sand beaches all day and then roll them bones all night. Maybe I'll meet some local young lady who's got a hankerin' for a mainline hunk like myself. We'll sip martinis and piña coladas as I bet on black and show my prowess at the poker tables. If that doesn't get me an open invitation for romance, then I don't know what will! Hell, yeah! Hawaii!

Huh? What are you talking about? Are you serious?! Hawaii doesn't have any form of legal gambling? Then why the heck does anybody go there? I mean, perfect beaches and weather and scenic beauty are fine, but where are the slots? The poker rooms? The blackjack tables?

Fine, fine. Then how about Utah? It's got the desert, like Nevada, but I hear it's a little cooler there. There are all these beautiful mountains and that, what's it called, Great Salt Lick? And they've got that Moron Tabernacle Choir in case I want to hear some music. Yep. Utah. That's the place. I'll meet some nice wholesome girls during the day, win some big bucks in the keno parlor, head over to the craps table, and then go home with lady luck—if she's willing. Know what I mean? Wink, wink. Nudge, nudge.

What? Oh, you've got to be kidding me! Utah doesn't have any legalized gaming either? What the heck is wrong with that state? What? Do they think there's something immoral about gambling or something? What a bunch of uptight prudes.

Fine. Fine. What a pain. Sin City it is.

PART 6:

BE A SPORT: SPORTSBOOK AND HORSERACING

IT'S A PURELY UNSCIENTIFIC GUESS, but the nation's number-one form of illegal gambling is probably sports betting. Offices in America that lack football or basketball pools are the exception and not the rule. Good friends who are also fans of opposing teams don't hesitate to put their money where their mouths are when it comes to team loyalty. And why shouldn't you bet on sporting events? Athletes make obscene amounts of money. Shouldn't you be entitled to some as well?

Sportsbooks are a legal way to place wagers on professional and collegiate competition, and millions visit them each year. You can bet on practically every sport and even on events within match-ups: the number of field goals in a football game, the number of struck-out batters in a baseball game, the number of three-point shots during the Final Four.

And long before there were Packers, Raiders, Saints, and Titans, there was horseracing. And as long as there has been horseracing, there have been folks who blow off work and head down to the track to wager money they can't afford to lose on their imagined equine expertise. So, what do you need to know to transform from fan to fan with some money in his or her pockets? Read on.

90: READY, SET, BET: HOW BETTING LINES WORK

Bragging rights are great, but nothing beats winning big bucks because you put money on the faith you have in a favorite team. Wagering on sporting events is a billion-dollar industry in Las Vegas alone. If you were to factor in all of the illegal betting that goes on across the country—football pools, visits to local bookies—then the money that changes hands following significant sports events probably rivals the national debt.

Casinos make money from vigorish—or a commission—on every bet made, so it's in their best interest to encourage as much betting as possible. Blind loyalty will only go so far. If wagers were based simply on who wins a competition, then sooner or later reality would set in and consistently losing teams wouldn't attract much action. Casinos would lose money, and they don't much like to do that. Think about it: The "vig" on bets is usually $1. If only the winning teams receive wagers, the sportsbook would dole out a lot of money to winners and not even come close to making it up with the vig. But if just as many people are betting on the losers, then they make the vig—plus they get to keep the losers' money. That's why casinos set a "line" for a multitude of sporting events.

The line is a handicapping device that equalizes the risk of a wager, making it likely that the amounts bet on each team will be about equal. The betting line will fluctuate right up to the start of a game. If a last-minute report indicates that torrential rain will fall throughout a game, then the line could be changed if one of the teams traditionally plays very well or very poorly during monsoon season. If a key starting player for one of the teams is injured or suspended, then that likely will change the betting line. If one team in a match-up attracts significantly more betting activity than another, then the line may be changed to encourage more wagering on the other team.

The two different types of betting lines in most Las Vegas sportsbooks are the point spread and the money line. The point spread is most popular for football and basketball wagers. In this type of bet, the underdog is given extra points so the bet depends not necessarily on which team wins, but on the adjusted outcome of the final score. A bet on the favored team will win only if that team beats the underdog by a total greater than the point spread. A wager on the underdog will make you money if that team wins or loses by less than the point spread.

Let's look at the example of a fictionalized football match-up. The Waukesha Wombats are favored over the Knox-ville Knuggets by ten points. The final score in this battle of titans is thirty-one to fourteen. The point spread adds ten points to the Knuggets's score, so the final "really" is thirty-one to twenty-four. The Wombats have won by seven points, not seventeen. So wagers on the Knuggets will be winners. Even though the Wombats win, wagers on them will be losers because the team didn't beat the point spread. The house edge on point-spread bets is around 4.54 percent.

The other line is the money line or simply the line. Instead of a point spread, the teams are balanced by odds. The money line penalizes you for betting on favorites by forcing you to make lay bets. Lay bets are when you risk more money than you'll win. If you bet on the favored team, you wager more money to win less. If you bet on the underdog instead, you wager less to win more. For example, if odds on the winner are six to five, then you have to bet $6 to win $5. On the other hand, if odds on the underdog, or "dog," team are eight to five, then a $5 bet would win $8 if the dog snags barking rights. The house edge on the money line bet is also around 4.54 percent.

Another type of bet you can make on most sporting events is the over/under. For this wager, you're betting on the total number of points scored in a game by both teams. If the over/under on a betting board is Womabats/Knuggets O/U 40 and the final score of the game is thirty-seven, then those who bet the score would be over forty would lose. Anyone who bet the score would be under forty would win.

One final thing to note about the sportsbook: at most casinos, you need to make your bets in $11 increments in order to adjust for the vigorish. If your bets aren't made in increments of eleven, then you could wind up not getting your full money's worth. Books round down bets not divisible by eleven.

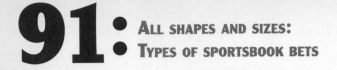

91: ALL SHAPES AND SIZES: TYPES OF SPORTSBOOK BETS

Without a doubt, the most popular sport for betting is football. Huge sums are placed on both college and professional match-ups. Because this type of sportsbook betting is so popular, there are a number of wagers you can make. You name the game, and it's assured that you can bet the point spread, line, and/or over/under on the outcome.

Bets on both college and NBA basketball games are also very popular in Las Vegas sportsbooks. The available bets are point spread and over/under. If you look at the betting board for a b-ball match-up, it will look something like this:

KNOXVILLE KNEE-CAPS
Waukesha Widgets +7
O/U 150

The team on top is the favorite. The team in capital letters is the home team. If you want to bet on the underdog, you might wager $11 that Waukesha will be triumphant. If the team wins, you win. If the team loses by six points or less, you win. Otherwise, you're a total loser. If you bet on the favorite, but Knoxville wins by six points or less, then you lose. If in the final score, Knoxville wins by exactly seven points, then it's considered a tie for bettors. You don't win anything, but you do get all your money back. If the final score of the game totals more than 150, then those who bet the score would be over 150 win, and those who bet it wouldn't, lose.

Baseball's popularity is slipping in the United States, and that carries over to sportsbooks. You can only bet on professional games, and typically, the only available bet is the money line, though some sportsbooks will offer over/under bets on occasion. The betting board on baseball looks like this:

Knoxville Knobodies - 7½
WAUKESHA WONDERBOYS 6½

Knoxville again is the favored team. You can tell because Knoxville's odds have a minus sign in front of them. The capital letters tip you off that the game is being played in Waukesha. Wagers on baseball are based on $5 bets. So in the above example, you'll win $5 for every $7.50 bet on the Knobodies, if the Knobodies win. If you bet on the Wonderboys to win, then you get $6.50 for every $5 you wager.

Betting on professional hockey is becoming increasingly popular in Las Vegas sportsbooks. Odds are listed as a point spread, like this:

Knoxville Knebbishes 2
WAUKESHA WOODENHEADS

Knoxville's the favorite, and the game is being played in Waukesha. If you bet on the favorite, and Knoxville wins by three or more goals, you win. If they only win by one goal, you lose. If you're a Woodenhead fan and choose to bet on Waukesha, then you'll win if the Woodenheads win or lose by only one goal. Some sportsbooks also will offer over/under bets on professional hockey match-ups.

Boxing matches are also a big sportsbook draw. They use the money line. So the betting board might look like this:

Tiny Ted 11
Battlin' Bill 8

Like baseball, the money line in boxing is based on $5 bets. In the above match-up, Tiny Ted is the favorite. You'll have to bet $11 to win $5 if you bet on the favorite. If you think Battlin' Bill has a good shot at being a contender, then you'll get $8 for every $5 bet on him, should he win.

92: PARLAY VOUS FRANÇAIS?: THE ART OF THE PARLAY AND ASSORTED OTHER BETS

Parlays are the sucker bets of sports betting. It's no wonder one of them is called a "teaser." Parlays are bets on more than one game at a time. To collect, you must win all of the bets. Your odds of winning, say, three games are lower than your odds of winning a wager placed on just one. If you win two of the wagers but lose one, you lose the whole enchilada. And it gets worse. Parlay odds are skewed heavily from true odds.

For example, the true odds on a two-team parlay are three to one. But the typical sportsbook payout is thirteen to five. A three-team parlay should pay out seven to one, but the book odds are typically six to one. The more games you parlay, the bigger the advantage for the sportsbook.

You bet on an enhanced point spread on two or more games for so-called teaser bets. For example, if the point spread on two teams is seven, then the teaser card will allow you to add or subtract a few points on either side of seven. It's a "tease" because enhanced point spread looks mighty attractive. But teaser bets pay off at lower odds than other parlay cards. And again, you need to win all of the games on your card to win anything at all. You're better off making individual wagers on the different games.

Another type of bet offered for most sports at sportsbooks is so-called props—or proposition bets, basically micro-betting. For a football game, you can make props on how many field goals will be made during the course of a game or on the number of completed passes. In baseball, you might bet on the number of home runs. Props on a basketball game include the number of three-point shots you believe will be made. Proposition bets typically are over/under bets. For example, the sportsbook might decide three field goals will be attempted during a football match-up. You can bet the actual number will be higher or lower than three, and if you're right, you win.

Finally, most sportsbooks have futures bets you can make on the outcome of an entire season. You can place a bet at the beginning of baseball season, for example, wagering that the Chicago Cubs will finally go to the World Series. You'd probably get very good odds for that one. But if the Cubbies make a tremendous showing in the National League throughout the year, odds will be adjusted throughout the season. If you placed your bet early, though, then your faith and prayers will be rewarded handsomely. If the Cubs win the pennant, the payout will be based on the odds at the time of your wager.

93: BE A SPORT: TOP TIPS ON WINNING AT THE SPORTSBOOK

When you bet on a particular sport, there are many factors you need to keep in mind. If it's football, you need to know if the match-up is just another game or a classic rivalry. A team having an awful season can still come through during a big rivalry because history will be an X-factor. If it's hockey, you need to know if the star player has been spending an awful lot of time in the penalty box lately. If the powers that be are coming down on him, his play could be more cautious. You need to consider these micro-factors, but there are certain tips that are helpful, regardless of the sport or the import of the match-up. Gambling expert J. Edward Allen offers several in his book, *How to Win at Sports Betting*.

Bet on sports events to make money. Period. If you're placing money on a game because you can't enjoy a match-up without something riding on it, then you probably need help. Gambling is exciting, yes. But you have even less control over a sporting event taking place 1,000 miles away than you do over a casino's wheel of fortune. Maybe you really do have a touch of telekinesis that allows you to slow down the wheel when it's most beneficial to you. But you're not going to have enough powers of persuasion to alter the course of 350-pound running backs.

Bet on games you believe you can win, based on your intimate knowledge of players and external conditions. Don't make a bet on the early, afternoon, and late games just because you want to have the chance to see action all day. Gambling is entertaining, but it's not strictly entertainment. It's not Monopoly. You're using real money—real money that you bust your butt all week to make. Use it wisely.

Bet with your head, not with your heart. If you're a graduate of the University of Tennessee, Knoxville, then don't bet on the Vols just because they're "your" team. Sure, they won the Sugar Bowl in 1998. But several lackluster seasons followed. You need to place bets based on a team's performance. Period. Loyalty is great. Feel free to tell your friends about all of the reasons beyond the team's control that it's not doing so well this season. Make impassioned "just wait'll next year" speeches. But don't put your hard-earned money on a high-pressure game.

When it comes to betting on sports, don't be a fan. Be a fan in your "real" life. Make your head a walking encyclopedia of stats on the Waukesha Wombats. But being a fan could cause you not to bet against Waukesha, even when you know they're bound to lose to the Walla Walla Washingtonians. The reason sportsbooks make money is in large part due to blind loyalty by fans. For that matter, being too attached to a particular team may cause you not to pay attention to other match-ups that could earn you big returns. Again, that's the reason you're betting in the first place . . . to make money.

Don't make bets thinking that they will add confidence to your favorite team. You love the Knoxville Knuggets, so you plunk down $200 on their big game against the Wichita Linemen, even though the Linemen are highly favored. Hey, you think, it'll help the team to know fans are rooting for 'em. Well, no, it won't. The team won't know that you wagered more money than you could afford on them. And even if they did, it's unlikely that would be the deciding factor to make the Knuggets beat the odds. The only thing this put-your-money-where-your-mouth-is philosophy will affect is your billfold.

And finally, ignore tips you've got to pay for. If you're with your buddies around the water cooler and one of them starts talking about a lock one team has on the season, you can just blow him off. But sports magazines and papers and Web sites sometimes offer you "can't miss" season tips for the low, low price of like, fifty bucks. Don't buy into these scams. Save your money. Get your own—free—education, and then bet with your head throughout the season.

94: AND THEY'RE OFF: HOW TO READ A RACING SHEET

Horseracing is called the sport of kings—probably because only kings can afford to own racehorses. But just plain folks can get in on horseracing action at tracks and off-track betting parlors across the country. Betting on races can be daunting to beginners, in part because racing tip sheets seem impossible to read. So some folks just bet on whatever horse "feels" right to them. But the sheets offer a wealth of good information, and if you learn how to read them, you can increase your chance of winning.

First of all, let's look at the common abbreviations. The tip sheets have to cram an awful lot of information into a short space, so they use more abbreviations than the federal government. The abbreviations refer to five characteristics: horse's color, horse's sex, track sizes, track conditions, and race types.

Common abbreviations referring to color are: b, which stands for bay; blk, black; br, brown; ch, chestnut; gr, gray; and ro, roan. Things get pretty personal when it comes to a horse's sex: c stands for colt, a male horse four years old or younger; f, filly, a female horse four years old or younger; g, gelding, a castrated male; h, horse, a male five years old or older; m, mare, a female five years or older or a younger female horse that has been bred; r, ridgeling, a male whose testicles aren't fully descended.

Track-size abbreviations are pretty straightforward: ½ means one-half mile; 5/8, five-eights of a mile; ¾, three-quarters of a mile; 7/8, seven-eights of a mile; and 1, one mile. Here are the abbreviations you're likely to see for track conditions: ft, which means fast, the best condition; gd, good, a few wet spots; sy, sloppy, puddles, but a firm base; my, muddy, wet with a soft base; hy, heavy, somewhere between muddy and good. Finally, let's look at race types, often called race conditions—which will be explained more fully in the next point: CD means conditioned race; 5000CL, claiming race (the number indicates the value on this horse); OP, optional; EC, early closer; LC, late closer; STK, stakes race; FUT, futurity; FFA, free-for-all; INV, invitational; OPN, open; HC, handicap; MDN, maiden; QUA, qualifying race; MAT, matinee race.

OK, now you know what all of those funky abbreviations mean, so let's look at a typical—though in this case made-up—racing sheet for a particular horse:

2 LUCKY BREAK Murn, Marty (175-30-52-26)   Life: 20
  4 4 1$160,000
bk c 3 Yo Daddy-Yo Mama-Makin' It Great   Tr-Nicole
  Gabrielle (81-17-9-15)
Or-Joe Carmean, Seaford, DE   Br-Ben Malisow

This is the information you'll see at the top of the sheet.
This horse's name is Lucky Break, and he's the number two
horse today. The jockey is Marty Murn, and the numbers in
parentheses are the number of times he's ridden this year
(175), followed by the number of first-, second-, and third-
place finishes he's had this year. The next block of information tells us that Lucky Break has been in twenty races, of
which he's won four, come in second in four, and come in third
in one. His lifetime money earnings total is $160,000.

The next line tells us the horse is a three-year-old black
colt. His father, or sire, was Yo Daddy. His mother, or dam, was
Yo Mama, and Makin' It Great sired Yo Mama. Lucky Break's
trainer is Nicole Gabrielle, and her record is in parentheses.
The last line of this portion of the sheet contains the name of
the horse's owner, Joe Carmean, and breeder, Ben Malisow.

The next lines on a racing sheet are the past-performance
lines, and they look like gibberish at first. Here's what the
left side of a typical past-performance line looks like:

28Oct04 FL ft78   INV HCP $15,000   1 26 55 123 154

The last time Lucky Break raced was on October 28, 2004, at the Finger Lakes track in upstate New York. It was a fast track, and the temperature during the race was seventy-eight degrees. It was an invitational handicap race with a $15,000 purse. The track was one-mile long, and the numbers that follow "1" are the time in seconds of the leading horse—which may or may not have been Lucky Break—at the quarter-, half-, and three-quarter-mile mark. The final number is the winning horse's time, in seconds. Most of the time, you'll see superscript numbers above these last four figures. They indicate fifths of seconds.

The right half of a past-performance line looks like this:

4 4¾ 2½ 1½　1½ 1¾　26 154　Becker, D.　*1.40　Lucky Break, Rat Pack, Ol' Blue Eyes

Lucky Break started in the fourth position. At the quarter-mile, he was fourth, three-quarter length from the leader. At the half, he was second, one-half length from the leader. At the three-quarter post, Lucky Break was in the lead, one-half length ahead. The next numbers show where Lucky Break was positioned entering the home stretch and where he finished the race. The superscript numbers refer to the lengths ahead Lucky Break was. In the above example, Lucky Break took twenty-six seconds to finish the last quarter-mile of the race, and finished it in a total of 154 seconds.

The jockey's name for this race was D. Becker, and 1.40 refers to the payout for this horse in the win pool. The asterisk means Lucky Break was the favorite. Finally, we learn that Lucky Break was the winner of this race, followed by Rat Pack and Ol' Blue Eyes.

95: STAKE OUT: TYPES OF RACES

Now that you're armed with a decipherable racing sheet, you're on the way to the track. But not all races are created equal because not all horses are created equal. There are five basic types, or classes, of horseracing, which reflect the quality of the horses involved: claiming races, maiden races, allowance races, handicap races, and stakes races.

Claiming races are the most common. The purses are small, and the horses are the lowest in quality of any you'll encounter at the track. Any horse entered in a claiming race can be bought, or claimed, by anyone for the claiming price listed in a program. Most of the time, it's a stable or professional horseman who buys them, but every so often, an amateur will see a man about a horse.

A horse must be bought prior to a race, and it becomes the new owner's property. But the purse will belong to the previous owner following this initial race. For bettors, it's difficult to handicap, or figure out a good strategy, for claiming races because the quality of the horses is uniformly low and difficult to predict. As a rule of thumb, you can figure that a higher claiming price reflects a better class of horse.

Maiden races are a cut above claiming races and are the class in which future stars of the track often begin their careers. Horses in maiden races have not yet won a race and are too valuable for owners to run in a claiming race. In allowance races, a variety of elements are factored in, from races run to money won in the past. Horses are assigned weight allowances to help balance the quality of individual horses. Allowance races cover a gambit of purses, horse ages, and horse classes.

Handicap races are for near-top-level horses and offer large purses. The track handicapper learns everything there is to know about the various horses in order to assign weight allowances to them and equalize their performances. This makes the races more exciting for bettors because, in theory, any of these top-quality horses could be a winner. And finally, there are stakes races. These feature the best of the best. This class of race features the competitions with which even disinterested folks are familiar: the Kentucky Derby, the Preakness, the Belmont Stakes—the events that make up horseracing's Triple Crown.

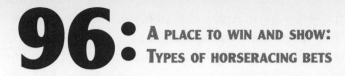

96: A PLACE TO WIN AND SHOW: TYPES OF HORSERACING BETS

And they're off! Ah, some of the most exciting words in all of sports. The thrill of the clanging bells and lifting gates . . . thoroughbreds charging at eye-popping speeds . . . the thunder of hoofs and rain of flying sod churned up by equine competitors. Oh yes, and a mint julep for good measure. And even if you don't really get the full effect of the races because you're watching them in a sportsbook rather than live at the track, horseracing remains a powerful spectacle . . . and it doesn't hurt the excitement factor if you've got some money riding on the race. Horseracing offers a variety of bets.

You can place a straight win bet, which means you bet a particular horse will win a particular race. For a place bet you wager your horse will finish first or second, and if you bet on a horse to show, this is called an across-the-board bet because you're wagering your horse will finish first, second, or third. You can bet on more than one horse in a race.

Bets can also be placed on the order of a race's top finishers. A quinella bet allows you to wager on which horses will come in first and second, and the order doesn't matter. An exacta is a similar bet, except that you only win if you correctly predict the order of the top-two finishers. A trifecta is similar to an exacta.

You win if you correctly predict the top three finishers in the order they finish the race. And a superfecta is a wager that predicts the top-four finishers in the correct order.

Horseracing bets don't have to be limited to one race. The daily double is a wager predicting the winners of the first two races of the day. Both horses have to win for you to collect. Most tracks also offer triples, a bet predicting the winners of three consecutive races. Once again, all three must win in order for you to collect. You can make an absolute fortune with the pick six bet, which is made on the finishers in six consecutive races—typically the last six races of the day.

THE BIG CASINO . . .
WHAT YOU DIDN'T KNOW ABOUT DEATH IN
VEGAS AND VEGAS-RELATED DEATH

If someone known to the Rat Pack passed away, Frank Sinatra and his pals said they'd bought the big casino or simply the big "c." The Pack was all about life and living big, and death had no place in their world. Nonetheless, it's not surprising that a place billed as the Entertainment Capital of the World would be the site of numerous star deaths nor should it be a shock that many stars call Las Vegas their eternal home.

Some Vegas-related stars died from old age, others from excess. And some died spectacularly in a hail of gunfire. Some famous deaths took folks who'd made their name in Sin City, while others died there because they had to die somewhere. And why not Vegas, baby?

97:
Hope I die 'fore I get old...
The Who's John Entwistle

For a city billed as the Entertainment Capital of the World, Las Vegas has been remarkably free of rock star deaths. It actually netted a rap star death first, when Tupac Shakur died there in 1996. Shakur was shot by unknown assailants after a Mike Tyson fight. It took until the twenty-first century for a rock 'n' roll giant to buy the big casino in Sin City. And it turned out to be a rather surprising death to boot.

The Who's resident crazy, alcohol-and-drug-taking, party-hearty bad boy Keith Moon died in 1978. When he was alive, the manic and talented drummer always seemed like the id to the ego of his rhythm section colleague John Entwistle. Moon enjoyed elegant pursuits like public nudity and hostelry destruction, while Entwistle was known as "The Ox" because he was so stoic and solid.

That's not to say he couldn't rock. Entwistle's other nickname was "Thunderfingers." All you have to do to find out how he got that nickname is listen to the bass solos on "My Generation." In addition to his playing, Entwistle wrote such Who fan favorites as "Boris the Spider," "Heaven and Hell," and "My Wife."

Fortunately or unfortunately, Entwistle belied the message of "My Generation." He was eligible for senior citizen discounts when he died on June 27, 2002 at the age of fifty-seven. Appropriately, he died in his room at Las Vegas's Hard Rock Hotel and Casino, on the eve of a concert tour that was to begin at the hotel. Initial reports indicated that The Ox's death was the result of a massive heart attack. That too seemed appropriate: a respectable death for a respectable man.

The shock came a month later, when a Las Vegas medical examiner reported that Entwistle did, indeed, die of a massive heart attack . . . brought on by cocaine use. Cocaine? John Entwistle? Fans couldn't believe it. Cocaine was the purview of the late, great Keith Moon, not Thunderfingers. Entwistle was an art lover—he designed The Who's "Paint by Numbers" album—and a quiet, gentle man.

But it was true, and Las Vegas had its first rock star drug death. The concert at the Hard Rock was canceled. But after Entwistle died, group leader Pete Townshend didn't claim The Who would disband, as he did after Keith Moon died. The tour continued, on schedule, with someone else playing bass. But no one—and this the band admitted—could ever replace the strong, quiet presence of The Ox nor the booming volume of Thunderfingers.

98: MONEY HONEY: COL. TOM PARKER

The man who would rule the King of Rock 'n' Roll using the name Col. Tom Parker was born Andreas Cornelius van Kujik in Breda, Holland. He most likely entered the United States as an illegal immigrant. But in classic American rags-to-riches fashion, van Kujik made it big in his new country. He became Elvis Presley's manager and probably the most famous—some Elvis fans would say most infamous—talent manager ever.

Van Kujik arrived in America in 1929 and joined the Army. He took the name "Tom Parker" from his commanding officer. By the mid-1930s, Parker was in Pensacola, Florida and found his true calling, as a carnival huckster with Royal American Shows. Then he moved to Tampa and gained local fame as a colorful dogcatcher. Parker talked his way into show business management, governing the careers of country greats Hank Snow and Eddy Arnold.

Parker became Elvis's manager in 1956. His first act was to have RCA buy out Elvis's contract at Memphis's Sun Records for a whopping $30,000—an astronomical sum for a fledgling talent in those days. Parker always was good at making himself and "his boy" wealthy. But some believe

Parker was also a driving force in compromising Elvis's artistic integrity. It's enough to know that Elvis made all of those horrible films in the 1960s because the Colonel thought they were a good idea.

Parker also controlled Elvis's musical output. He made an exclusive deal with the music publishing company Hill and Range. Under it, anyone who wrote Elvis songs had to write them for Hill and Range. Writers gave up half the rights to their songs—and half their composer's royalties. Those royalties lined Elvis and the Colonel's pockets. For most songwriters, it was a small price to pay in order to have a tune recorded by the King of Rock 'n' Roll.

Of course, the arrangement also meant that Hill and Range rarely got the pick of the songwriting litter. Elvis gained fame with such for-Elvis originals as "Heartbreak Hotel," but during his movie years, he recorded such "classics" as "There's No Room to Rhumba in a Sports Car" and "Yoga Is as Yoga Does."

Elvis fans tend to hate Parker because they believe he drained Elvis's talent throughout the bulk of "his boy's" career. Some fans also blame the Colonel for Elvis's early death, which followed nearly ceaseless, grueling concert tours. The Colonel's boy died on August 16, 1977. Supposedly, when informed of the news, the Colonel merely responded by saying, "This doesn't change anything." And in a sense, he was right. Elvis earned a lot more money after he passed away than he did in the days when he was alive to spend—and to give away—money hand over fist.

Col. Parker outlived Elvis by nearly twenty years. He died in Las Vegas's Valley Hospital Medical Center of complications from a stroke on January 21, 1997. He was eighty-seven. In his final years, Parker occasionally advised the Las Vegas Hilton on entertainment. But mostly he just gambled. The Colonel didn't drink or smoke, but he loved table games. Despite countless offers to tell his story, Col. Tom Parker never did write an autobiography, and he rarely gave interviews. No one will ever know if he felt responsible for Elvis's fame . . . or for his untimely death.

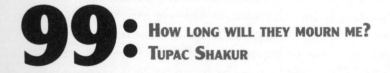

99: HOW LONG WILL THEY MOURN ME? TUPAC SHAKUR

Tupac Shakur was born on June 16, 1971, the son of a Black Panther named Afeni Shakur (born Alice Faye Williams). Afeni was in the Women's House of Detention in New York's Greenwich Village for most of her pregnancy, and she feared she wouldn't make it to term due to malnourishment. Afeni was married to Lumumba Shakur, but—convinced that Afeni's pregnancy wasn't his doing—he divorced her. Tupac Shakur grew up not knowing who his father was.

Shakur grew up all over New York and Baltimore. At seventeen he moved with his family to Marin City, California. From a young age, Shakur was a sensitive boy who grew up in a world filled with drugs and crime. He acted for the first time at age twelve, in a Harlem theater group. He wrote his first rap while living in Baltimore. In California, he quickly got involved in the underground rap scene. While on tour as a dancer with Digital Underground—whose "Humpty Dance" was a huge hit—he learned his mother had become addicted to crack. For years, the two rarely spoke.

Shakur himself was no stranger to illegal activity. During a celebration of Marin City's fiftieth anniversary in 1992, Shakur got into a confrontation with some old acquaintances. During the ensuing melee, a six-year-old boy was shot in the head. No criminal charges were filed against the rapper, but he was subjected to a civil suit. Another suit that year alleged a young black man killed her policeman husband as a result of listening to Shakur's music. When Shakur moved to Atlanta for a quieter life, he was arrested for allegedly shooting two white, off-duty police officers.

Despite all of the trouble in which Shakur became embroiled, he found time to be a successful and both critically and popularly successful actor and rapper. His debut release, 1991's "2Pacalypse Now," reached #13 on the R & B charts. "Strictly 4 My N.I.G.G.A.Z.," from 1993, reached #4. Shakur's first film role was in 1992's *Juice*, followed by *Poetic Justice*, which starred Janet Jackson. A double threat in 1994's *Above the Rim*, he was one of the leads in the film, and the soundtrack album he recorded for the film became the rapper's first R & B #1. In 1995, the last full year of his life, Shakur's albums were topping both the R & B and the pop charts.

On the night Shakur was gunned down in Las Vegas, the least interesting aspect of the evening was the Mike Tyson fight the rapper attended. Tyson immediately knocked down a hapless Bruce Seldon. After the fight, Shakur and Death Row Records founder Suge Knight headed out for a drive, with Knight at the wheel. It was around 11 P.M. on September 7, 1996.

Knight pulled off of Las Vegas Boulevard onto Flamingo Avenue. Presumably, he was heading for Club 662, which he owned. Knight and Shakur were sitting at a traffic light. The cross street was Paradise. A late-model white Cadillac with California plates pulled up next to Knight's BMW. The Cadillac's occupants fired into the BMW between ten and fifteen times at point blank range. Two bullets ripped through Shakur's chest. He lost a lot of blood during his quick trip to University Medical Center. Shakur lingered for six days in the hospital, drifting in and out of consciousness. But he died of respiratory failure and cardiopulmonary arrest at 4:03 P.M. on Friday, September 13.

Shakur's death in Las Vegas was a shock, but it wasn't totally unexpected, even to the rapper. His work was filled with songs bearing titles like "If I Die Tonight" and "How Long Will They Mourn Me?" The answer to that question is impossible to determine. Nearly a decade after his death,

Shakur's unpublished poems and raps continue to be released. Biographies of the rapper continue to be released. No one remembers Mike Tyson's pre-ear-biting bout from September of 1996, but fans of Tupac Shakur will never forget what else happened that night on a Las Vegas street named for the Fabulous Flamingo, brainchild of the original Vegas gangsta, Bugsy Siegel.

100: ELIZABETH, THIS IS THE BIG ONE, HONEY! REDD FOXX

John Elroy Sanford was born on December 9, 1922 in St. Louis. His ruddy complexion earned him the nickname "Redd" at a young age, and he took the surname "Foxx" from major league baseball player Jimmie Foxx. After a stint in a band, Foxx moved to New York and palled around with and constantly cracked up Malcolm Little, the future Malcolm X. Foxx's natural humor led him to become a professional comedian on the so-called Chitlin Circuit of black nightclubs.

Foxx's fame grew once he started recording albums of his routines in the 1950s. Then, in 1972, he was tapped to play irascible junk dealer Fred Sanford—note that the character shared Foxx's real last name.

During the five years Foxx was on the show, *Sanford and Son* was a huge hit, usually landing in the top ten. At one point, the show ran twice a week on NBC. Despite its popularity, the Hollywood establishment barely recognized *Sanford and Son*. It won a single Emmy, for Achievement in Video Tape Editing. The Golden Globe Awards smiled on Foxx, though. He won the Globe for Best TV Actor in a Musical or Comedy in 1973 and was nominated in 1974, 1975, and 1976.

Foxx left the show in 1977, lured away by ABC, which promised the comedian a huge salary and his own variety show, *The Redd Foxx Comedy Hour*. The show lasted less than a season. After that, Foxx did not go gently into that good night. He went to Vegas, baby! He headlined for years, occasionally trying new television series that fared no better than *The Redd Foxx Comedy Hour*.

After starring with Della Reese in Eddie Murphy's not-very-good 1989 film, *Harlem Nights*, CBS signed Foxx and Reese to co-star in a new sitcom, *The Royal Family*, in 1991. On *Sanford and Son*, Foxx's signature schtick was his character's response to news he didn't want to hear. Fred Sanford clutched his chest, stumbled backwards and spoke dramatically to his deceased wife: "Oh, this is the big one! You hear that Elizabeth? I'm coming to join you, honey!" Well, "the big one" hit Foxx on the set of *The Royal Family*. Della Reese prayed over Foxx, begging him to live, but the sixty-eight-year-old comedian was dead of a heart attack.

Foxx was buried in Las Vegas, his adopted home. The house he owned in Sin City, which has become a commercial business since Foxx's death, is said to be haunted by the ghost of the foul-mouthed—but loveable—comedian who shattered racial and cultural barriers throughout his life.

101: Don't call me Bugsy: Benjamin "Bugsy" Siegel

It's entirely fitting that the one-time president of Murder Incorporated didn't die peacefully in his sleep. It's just too bad that Benjamin—don't call me "Bugsy"—Siegel didn't die in Sin City, the town he helped develop into a sophisticated playground for adults. Instead, he died in another town noted for sin and sensationalism: Los Angeles.

Bugsy was born in 1905 in Manhattan's Lower East Side. By the age of fourteen, he had his own street gang. Not long after, he became fast friends with Meyer Suchowljansky, who went by the name Meyer Lansky. These adolescents became known as the "Bug and Meyer Mob," and they carried out murder contracts for New York bootlegging outfits. Bugsy most likely gained his nickname because he sometimes acted strangely and really, really loved violence. He was "buggy," as in "crazy." Siegel, Lansky, and other friends—such as Charles "Lucky" Luciano—became kings of the New York underworld. One of the group's rackets was a horseracing wire service. Bugsy first went to Las Vegas because of that wire service, which was run illegally in every other state that used it.

Bugsy divided his time between Hollywood and Las Vegas and divided his personal life among several starlets, the most prominent being Virginia Hill. One of his male friends was Billy Wilkerson, founder of the *Hollywood Reporter*. Wilkerson had an idea for putting a place in Vegas that would force Wild-West relics like the Last Frontier out of business: a truly fancy and sophisticated gambling palace. Bugsy glommed quickly onto the idea. He figured it would take about a million bucks to build the Flamingo, which he named after the colorful birds at Miami's Hialeah horseracing track. To say that the Flamingo suffered cost overruns would be an understatement. Bugsy bought materials at exorbitant prices, and often those materials were stolen from the job site and resold to Siegel. That initial, million-dollar estimate was surpassed quickly. Bugsy's financing, which came from his "business associates," ballooned to $6 million. It would be another understatement to say that mob leaders were not particularly pleased with this turn of events.

The Flamingo opened on December 26, 1946. It was a disaster. The Flamingo was a turkey. The weather was poor, so most of the expected Hollywood royalty stayed home. Gamblers gave the house a beating, and then to add insult to injury, they had to take their winnings across the street to the El Rancho and the Last Frontier—the very joints Bugsy wanted to eclipse—because the Flamingo's hotel rooms weren't finished. Within days, the Flamingo was a further $300,000 in debt. Bugsy closed it down and scrambled to complete its accommodations. It reopened on March 1, 1947, with the Andrews Sisters headlining.

The Flamingo began to show signs of turning a profit. But it was too late for Benjamin "Bugsy" Siegel. Even though he moved constantly between Las Vegas and Los Angeles and often changed the locks on his doors, his former associates caught up with him on June 20, 1947.

Bugsy was alone in Virginia Hill's Beverly Hills mansion, leafing through the *Los Angeles Times*. Nine shots rang out. One slug from a .30-caliber Army carbine went through the back of Bugsy's neck and destroyed his pretty face. Another knocked his right eye fifteen feet across the room. Bugsy was gone, replaced by Gus Greenbaum. Greenbaum managed to make the Flamingo a huge success right away. Ironically, he too met a grim fate. He and his wife were visiting Phoenix in 1958 when their throats were cut. The murders of the Greenbaums and of Siegel never were solved.

BIBLIOGRAPHY

Allen, J. Edward. *The Basics of Winning Caribbean Stud Poker and Let It Ride.* (New York: Cardoza Publishing, 2003).

Allen, J. Edward. *The Basics of Winning Keno.* (New York: Cardoza Publishing, 2003).

Allen, J. Edward. *The Basics of Winning Poker.* (New York: Cardoza Publishing, 2003).

Allen, J. Edward. *How to Win at Sports Betting.* (New York: Cardoza Publishing, 1990).

Begun, Abbey. *Gambling: Crime or Recreation?* (Farmington Hills, MI: Gale Group, 2000). *http://casinocity.com*

Coakley, Deirdre, Hank Greenspun, Gary C. Beard, and the Staff of the Las Vegas Sun. *The Day the MGM Grand Hotel Burned.* (Secaucus, NJ: Lyle Stuart Inc., 1982).

Coffey, Frank. *The Complete Idiot's Guide to Elvis.* (New York: Alpha Books, 1997).

Davis, Sammy Jr., Jane and Burt Boyar. *Yes I Can: The Story of Sammy Davis, Jr.* (New York: Farrar, Straus & Giroux, 1965).

Editors of *Vibe. Tupac Shakur.* (New York: Three Rivers Press, 1998).

Eisler, Kim Isaac. *Revenge of the Pequots: How a Small Native American Tribe Created the World's Most Profitable Casino.* (New York: Simon & Schuster, 2001).

Freedland, Michael. *All the Way: A Biography of Frank Sinatra 1915–1998*. (New York, St. Martin's, 1997).

Garrison, Omar. *Howard Hughes in Las Vegas*. (New York: Dell Publishing, 1970).

Glazer, Andrew N.S. *Casino Gambling the Smart Way: How to Make More Money and Have More Fun in any Game You Choose*. (Franklin Lakes, NJ: Career Press, 1999).

Hayes, Justin Cord. "Are You Afraid of Ghost Stories? Encounters with the Specters of Haunted Las Vegas," *Las Vegas Life*, October 1997, pp. 34–37.

Kayser, Brian D. *Secrets of Winning Baccarat: Proven Strategies from 232 Shoes*. (New York: Cardoza, 2003).

Land, Barbara and Myrick Land. *A Short History of Las Vegas*. (Reno, NV: University of Nevada Press, 1999).

Lewisohn, Mark. *The Complete Beatles Chronicle: The Only Definitive Guide to the Beatles' Entire Career*. (London: Hamlyn, 2000).

McMillan, James B. Fighting Back: *A Life in the Struggle for Civil Rights*. (Reno, NV: University of Nevada Oral History Program, 1997).

Morris, Edmund. *Dutch: A Memoir of Ronald Reagan*. (New York: Modern Library, 1999).

Nelson, Andy. *Poker: 101 Ways to Win*. (Boulder, CO: PokerBook Press, 1994).

The Official Site of Redd Foxx. *www.cmgww.com/stars/foxx/foxx.html*.

The Online Museum of Transgender Artifacts. *http://members.aol.com/dianeh1962/TGMmain.html.*

Reber, Arthur S. *The New Gambler's Bible: How to Beat the Casinos, the Track, Your Bookie, and Your Buddies.* (New York: Crown Trade Paperbacks, 1996).

Sheehan, Jack E., Editor. *The Players: The Men Who Made Las Vegas.* (Reno, NV: University of Nevada Press, 1997).

Sternlieb, George and James W. Hughes. *The Atlantic City Gamble.* (Cambridge, MA: Harvard University Press, 1983).

Transhistory.org: Transsexual, Transgender, and Intersex History. *www.transhistory.org.*

Wong, Stanford. *Basic Blackjack.* (La Jolla, CA: Pi Yee Press, 1993).